teach® yourself

**quick fix
french grammar**

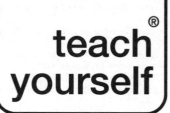

**quick fix
french grammar**

wendy bourbon with
duncan sidwell and elaine haviland

For over 60 years, more than
40 million people have learnt over
750 subjects the **teach yourself**
way, with impressive results.

be where you want to be
with **teach yourself**

For UK order queries: please contact Bookpoint Ltd, 130 Milton Park, Abingdon, Oxon OX14 4TD. Telephone: +44 (0) 1235 827720, Fax: +44 (0) 1235 400454. Lines are open 9.00–18.00, Monday to Saturday, with a 24-hour message answering service. You can also order through our website www.madaboutbooks.com

For USA order queries: please contact McGraw-Hill Customer Services, P.O. Box 545, Blacklick, OH 43004-0545, USA. Telephone: 1-800-722-4726. Fax: 1-614-755-5645.

For Canada order queries: please contact McGraw-Hill Ryerson Ltd, 300 Water St, Whitby, Ontario L1N 9B6, Canada. Telephone: 905 430 5000. Fax: 905 430 5020.

Long renowned as the authoritative source for self-guided learning – with more than 30 million copies sold worldwide – the *Teach Yourself* series includes over 300 titles in the fields of languages, crafts, hobbies, business, computing and education.

British Library Cataloguing in Publication Data: a catalogue entry for this title is available from The British Library.

Library of Congress Catalog Card Number: on file

First published in UK 2003 by Hodder Headline Ltd, 338 Euston Road, London, NW1 3BH.

First published in US 2003 by Contemporary Books, a Division of the McGraw-Hill Companies, 1 Prudential Plaza, 130 East Randolph Street, Chicago, IL 60601 USA.

The 'Teach Yourself' name is a registered trade mark of Hodder & Stoughton Ltd.

Copyright © 2003 Wendy Bourbon, Elaine Haviland, Duncan Sidwell

Typeset by Transet Limited, Coventry, England.
Printed in Great Britain for Hodder & Stoughton Educational, a division of Hodder Headline Ltd, 338 Euston Road, London NW1 3BH by Cox & Wyman Ltd, Reading, Berkshire.

Impression number	10 9 8 7 6 5 4 3 2
Year	2007 2006 2005 2004 2003

contents

introduction 1
nouns and articles
    01 the definite article   le, la, les   2
    02 the indefinite article   un, une, des   4
    03 uses of the articles   Elle a les cheveux longs.   6
    04 gender of nouns (1)   le russe, la banane   8
    05 gender of nouns (2)   -âge (m), -eau (m), -euse (f), -ère (f)   10
    06 nouns with two genders   le poste, la poste   12
    07 compound nouns   la belle-fille, le wagon-lit   14
    08 il est and **c'est**   Il est tard, c'est moi.   16
    09 the partitive article   du vin, de la confiture   18
prepositions
    10 simple prepositions (1)   après, avant, avec, chez, contre, dans   20
    11 simple prepositions (2)   depuis, derrière, devant, en, entre, envers, malgré   22
    12 simple prepositions (3)   par, parmi, pendant, pour, sans, sauf, sous, sur, vers   24
    13 the preposition **de**   la voiture de Paul, un verre de vin   26
    14 the preposition **à**   au cinéma, à l'heure   28
    15 complex prepositions   grâce à, à côté de   30
adjectives and adverbs
    16 possessive adjectives   mon livre, notre maison   32
    17 adjectives: agreement (1)   amusant, amusante   34
    18 adjectives: agreement (2)   heureux, heureuse   36
    19 adjectives: position   une jolie maison, un livre intéressant   38

20	demonstrative adjectives	ce, cet, cette, ces	40
21	adverbs (1): regular	sérieusement, absolument	42
22	adverbs (2): irregular	gentiment, bien	44
23	adverbs (3): position	Il travaille vite. J'ai trop mangé.	46
24	adjectives: comparison	plus … que, moins … que	48
25	adverbs: comparison	plus … que	50
26	adjectives: superlative	le/la plus …, le/la moins …, etc.	52
27	adverbs: superlative	le plus…, le moins…, le pis, etc.	54
28	indefinite adjectives and pronouns (1)	autre, certain, quelque, etc.	56
29	indefinite adjectives and pronouns (2)	chaque, quelque chose, etc.	58

verbs (1)

30	the verb	infinitive, regular, irregular	60
31	present tense (1): regular **-er** verbs	je porte, tu portes, il porte, etc.	62
32	present tense (2): **-er** verbs with stem changes	j'achète, nous achetons, etc.	64
33	present tense (3): regular **-ir** verbs	je finis, tu finis, il finit, etc.	66
34	present tense (4): regular **-re** verbs	je vends, tu vends, il vend, etc.	68
35	present tense (5): reflexive verbs	je me lève, tu te lèves, il se lève, etc.	70

pronouns

36	subject pronouns	je, tu, il, elle, on, nous, vous, ils, elles	72
37	subject pronoun: **on**	On va en ville? On est fatigués?	74
38	emphatic pronouns	moi, toi, lui, elle, etc.	76

39 possessive pronouns   le mien, la mienne, les miens, les miennes, etc.   78

40 demonstrative pronouns   celui, celle, ceux, celles   80

41 relative pronouns (1)   qui, que   82

42 relative pronouns (2)   dont, où   84

43 relative pronouns (3)   lequel, lesquels, laquelle, lesquelles   86

44 relative pronouns (4)   ce qui, ce que, ce dont   88

45 object pronouns (1)   me, te, le, la, les, lui, leur, etc.   90

46 object pronouns (2)   y, en   92

47 object pronouns (3): position   Elle les aide. Les aide-t-elle?   94

verbs (2)

48 irregular verbs: **avoir**   j'ai, tu as, il a, elle a, etc.   96

49 irregular verbs: **être**   je suis, tu es, il est, elle est, etc.   98

50 irregular verbs: **aller** and **faire**   je vais, je fais   100

51 irregular verbs: **mettre** and **prendre**   je mets, je prends   102

52 irregular verbs: **pouvoir** and **vouloir**   je peux, je veux   104

53 irregular verbs: **devoir** and **savoir**   je dois, je sais   106

54 verbs (more than one subject)   ma sœur et moi sortons   108

55 present participle   trouvant, sortant   110

56 imperative   continue, levez-vous   112

57 infinitive (1)   j'aime chanter, il veut venir   114

58 infinitive (2)   elle commence à le préparer   116

59 verb constructions with objects   j'attends Paul, je joue au golf   118

60 perfect tense (1)   j'ai acheté   120

61 perfect tense (2): with **être**   je suis allé(e)   122

62 perfect tense (3): reflexive
verbs   je me suis levé(e)   124

63 perfect tense (4): agreement   je les ai vus   126

64 imperfect tense   j'allais, il était   128

65 past tenses: perfect or
imperfect?   quand il est arrivé, elle mangeait   130

66 pluperfect tense   j'avais fini, elle était sortie   132

67 past historic tense   je parlai, il mangea   134

68 future tense   j'arriverai, il finira   136

69 future perfect tense   j'aurai acheté, vous aurez fait   138

70 conditional   je trouverais, il irait   140

71 conditional perfect   j'aurais acheté, vous auriez fait   142

72 using **si**   si tu viens, nous irons au cinéma   144

73 perfect infinitive   après avoir fini, après être
tombé(e)   146

74 passive   la pièce a été repeinte   148

75 present subjunctive   que j'attende   150

76 perfect subjunctive   que j'aie attendu   152

77 use of the subjunctive (1)   je veux que…   154

78 use of the subjunctive (2)   avant que… (ne), il faut que…   156

79 use of the subjunctive (3)   rien qui…, personne qui…,
quel que…   158

conjunctions

80 conjunctions (1)   donc, et, mais, ou, pourtant, etc.   160

81 conjunctions (2)   afin que, bien que, parce que, etc.   162

negatives

82 negatives (1)   ne … pas, ne … rien, ne …
jamais   164

83 negatives (2)   je n'ai pas compris   166

question forms

84 asking questions (1)   est-ce qu'il vient?   168

85 asking questions (2)   où? quand? comment?
combien? pourquoi? quel…?   170

86 asking questions (3)   lequel? qui…? que…?, etc.   172

numbers, dates and time

87 numbers (1)   un, deux, vingt, cent, etc.   174

88 numbers (2)   premier, une dizaine   176

89 fractions and decimals   une demie, la moitié, un quart   178

90 dimensions and distance   haut de…, long de…, etc.   180

91 telling the time   huit heures et demie, vingt
heures trente   182

92 days, dates and years   lundi le 15 février 1999   184

miscellaneous

93 depuis, il y a and **venir de**   depuis dix mois, il y a un an,
il vient de…   186

94 il y a   il y a sandwich pour toi   188

95 saying 'yes' and 'no'   oui, si, non   190

96 nationalities, etc.   la France, un Français, français   192

97 inversion   dit-il, a-t-il dit   194

98 'faux amis'   assister à   196

99 expressions of quantity   assez de, trop de   198

verbs followed by à/de   **200**

key to unit exercises   **203**

more practice   **211**

key to practice exercises   **259**

glossary   **269**

introduction

The purpose of this book

This book is designed to help you learn about the French language and how it is structured. It is divided into 99 units, each of which explains a particular grammar point. You will find related exercises on the practice pages which are located opposite the explanations for ease of reference. Answers to each of the exercises are provided at the end of the book, and the glossary explains the main grammatical terms used.

How to use this book

The contents page will help you to identify a grammar point you wish to practise. You do not need to work through the book in any particular order – you will find that each unit can be used independently as an introduction to new learning or for revision or reference. You may find it helpful to revisit a unit several times until you are able to complete the exercises without referring to the explanation. Writing the answers down and repeating them out loud can often aid learning.

Examples of more advanced grammar have been included to help you to develop your understanding of how the language works. As you progress, you will encounter many such points which you will find useful as your ability to manipulate the language grows.

Studying the grammar of a language can help you to identify the specific patterns and structures it contains. As a result, you will gradually be able to build up your understanding of how the language works, which will help you to use it effectively.

Bonne chance!

Nouns are words that name a person, an object or a concept. They can be singular or plural, and in French they have a gender.

A In French, nouns have a gender: they are either masculine or feminine. In dictionaries gender is shown by *nm* and *nf*. (*m*) or (*f*) are also used.

Masculine		Feminine	
le cinéma	*the cinema*	la voiture	*the car*
le dictionnaire	*the dictionary*	la liberté	*freedom*

B There are two words for *the* in the singular – **le** and **la**. These are called definite articles. Masculine nouns take **le**, feminine nouns take **la**.

• For all nouns beginning with a vowel (a, e, i, o, u) and most nouns beginning with an unsounded **h**, **le** and **la** are shortened to **l'**.

l'hôpital (*nm*)   *the hospital*   l'église (*nf*)   *the church*

To talk about more than one thing (masculine or feminine) you use **les**.

Masculine		Feminine	
les cinémas	*the cinemas*	les voitures	*the cars*
les livres	*the books*	les circonstances	*the circumstances*

C To make a noun plural an **-s** is usually added to it (not usually pronounced).

le document *the document* les documents *the documents*

However, some nouns have irregular plurals, and others do not change at all:

• Nouns ending in **-s**, **-x** or **-z** remain unchanged.

le bras	*the arm*	les bras	*the arms*
le prix	*the prize/price*	les prix	*the prizes/prices*

• Nouns ending in **-au** or **-eu** add an **-x**.

le bateau	*the boat*	les bateaux	*the boats*
le jeu	*the game*	les jeux	*the games*

• Nouns ending in **-al** or **-ail** drop their singular ending and add **-aux**.

le cheval	*the horse*	les chevaux	*the horses*
le travail	*the work*	les travaux	*the works*

But note:

le festival	*the festival*	**les festivals**	*the festivals*
un œil	*an eye*	les yeux	*the eyes*

exercise

Put *le*, *la*, or *l'* in front of the following nouns according to whether they are masculine (*nm*) or feminine (*nf*).

E.g. piscine (*nf*) *la* piscine → *swimming pool*

a supermarché (*nm*) *supermarket*
b banque (*nf*) *bank*
c pâtisserie (*nf*) *cake shop*
d fromage (*nm*) *cheese*

Like the word for *the*, the words for *a/an*, *some* or *any* vary according to the number and gender of the noun they relate to.

A The two words for *a* (or *an* before a vowel) are **un** and **une**. These are called indefinite articles. **Un** is used with masculine nouns, and **une** with feminine ones.

un journal	*a newspaper*
une veste	*a jacket*
une église	*a church*

B If you want to say *some books*, *any books* or even just *books* (rather than *a book*), you will need to use the word **des**. **Des** is used for both masculine and feminine nouns in the plural.

un journal	*a newspaper*	**des** journaux	*(some/any) newspapers*
une secrétaire	*a secretary*	**des** secrétaires	*(some/any) secretaries*
une école	*a school*	**des** écoles	*(some/any) schools*

Unlike **les**, **des** refers to an unspecified group of people, things or ideas. Compare:

J'ai vu **les** documents sur le bureau.	*I saw the documents on the desk.*
J'ai vu **des** documents sur le bureau.	*I saw documents (or some documents) on the desk.*

The word **des** cannot be left out, as *some* often is in English.

> J'ai acheté des sandwichs au supermarché.
>
> *I bought sandwiches (or some sandwiches) at the supermarket.*

C In English, we often use *any* after a question. This is expressed in French by **des**.

> Vous avez des enfants?
>
> *Have you got any children?*

D Des is replaced by **de** (or by **d'** before a noun beginning with a vowel or an unsounded **h**):

• after a negative:

> Je n'ai pas d'enfants.
>
> *I haven't got any children.*

• when an adjective precedes a plural noun:

> Ils vendent de belles voitures.
>
> *They sell (some) beautiful cars.*

> Ils ont de vieux meubles.
>
> *They've got (some) old furniture.*

exercise

Put *un* or *une* before the following nouns.

E.g. bateau (*nm*) → *un* bateau

a patron (*nm*) *boss*

b poste (*nf*) *post office*

c dîner (*nm*) *dinner*

d chambre (*nf*) *room*

e piano (*nm*) *piano*

f timbre (*nm*) *stamp*

French usage of the definite and indefinite articles differs in some ways from English usage.

A The French definite article is used as follows:

- with nouns being used in a general way

  Il s'intéresse à **la** pêche. *He's interested in fishing.*
  Le poisson est délicieux. *Fish is delicious.*

- to express price, rate or quantity

  C'est 1,8€ **le** kilo *It's 1.8 euros a kilo.*

- with parts of the body (rather than **son/sa**, etc.)

  Elle a **les** cheveux longs. *She has long hair.*
  Il s'est cassé **le** bras. *He broke his arm.*

However, the possessive adjective (**mon, ma, mes,** etc.) is used when an adjective qualifies the noun (except with **avoir** indicating possession, which always needs the definite article in sentences like those above).

> Elle a ouvert ses beaux *She opened her lovely blue*
> yeux bleus. *eyes.*

- with proper names used with an adjective, or with titles, ranks and professions

  La petite Marie s'est endormie. *Little Marie went to sleep.*
  C'est **le** colonel Chabart. *It's Colonel Chabart.*
  Le docteur Michelet est venu *Dr Michelet came to see*
  me voir. *me.*

- with the names of some festivals
  La Toussaint *All Saints' Day* **La** Pentecôte *Whitsun*

The definite article is not used with **Pâques** *Easter* and **Noël** *Christmas*.

- with nouns when they refer to a particular thing
  C'est à **la** page 5. *It's on page 5.*
  C'est **la** chambre numéro 18. *It's room 18.*

- with continents, countries, lakes, mountains, rivers, oceans, seas
  Le lac Léman est beau. *Lac Léman is beautiful.*

B The indefinite article means *a* or *an* and is used much as in English. Its plural form is **des** (*some, any* when plural). This is never omitted in French, although it can be in English.
  Elle a **un** nouveau bureau. *She's got a new office.*
  Des policiers l'ont arrêté. *Police officers arrested him.*

exercise

Put the correct article in front of each noun, using the English sentence as a guide to meaning.

E.g. _____ vieux Paul est en Italie. *Le* vieux Paul est en Italie.
  Old Paul's in Italy.

a _____ docteur Chabas est ici. *Dr Chabas is here.*

b Il a _____ cheveux blonds. *He's got fair hair.*

c _____ France est un grand pays. *France is a big country.*

d Elle s'est cassé _____ bras. *She's broken her arm.*

e _____vin blanc va bien avec _____ poulet. *White wine goes well with chicken.*

There are general rules that govern whether a noun is masculine or feminine in French. There are also exceptions to these rules.

A Most nouns falling into the following categories are *masculine*:

• human and animal males: l'homme *man*, le fermier *farmer*, le tigre *tiger*

• days, months, seasons, points of the compass: le mardi *Tuesday*, le mai *May*, l'automne *autumn*, l'ouest *west*

• countries and rivers not ending in -e: le Danemark *Denmark*, le Lot *the Lot* (but le Rhône, le Danube and le Mexique)

• languages: le français *French*, le russe *Russian*

• colours: le bleu *blue*, le jaune *yellow*

• metric weights and measures, cardinal numbers, fractions, letters: le litre *litre*, le trois *the number three*, un quart *a quarter*, le S *the letter S*

• trees and shrubs: le pommier *apple tree*; le lilas *lilac*

• fruits and vegetables not ending in -e: le citron *lemon*, le melon *melon*

• metals and minerals: le fer *iron*, le sel *salt*

B Nouns in the following categories are *feminine*:

• human and animal females: la femme *woman*, la lionne *lioness*

- female roles or occupational names: **l'actrice** *actress*, **la reine** *queen*. Many traditionally male roles and occupations can now be used with a feminine definite article for females where there is no female form of the noun: **la ministre** *minister*, **la docteur** *doctor*, **la professeur** *teacher*, **la médecin**
- countries and rivers ending in -e: **la Suisse** *Switzerland*, **la Loire** *the Loire*
- most fruit, flowers and vegetables: **la banane** *banana*, **la carotte** *carrot*
- school subjects, apart from specific languages (see above): **les langues** (*fpl*) *languages*, **la science** *science*
- arts, trades and sciences: **la sculpture** *sculpture*, **la physique** *physics*
- festivals: **la Toussaint** *All Saints' Day* (but **Pâques** (*nm*) *Easter* and the masculine expression **Joyeux Noël** *Happy Christmas*)

C Words for people can in some cases take either gender: **un(e) enfant** *child*, **un(e) élève** *pupil*, **le/la sans-emploi** *unemployed person*.

exercise

Give the gender (*le, la*) of the following nouns.

a lundi *Monday*   c rouge *red*

b musique *music*   d Chine *China*

The gender of a noun can also often be inferred from its endings. There are certain masculine and feminine forms for living things.

A Some noun endings for living creatures or people have a masculine form and a feminine form: **un chat** is a male cat, while **une chatte** is a female cat. Here is a table of these endings.

Masculine form		Feminine form	
-at	chat	-atte	chatte
-eur	vendeur	-euse	vendeuse
-eur	acteur	-rice	actrice
-er	épicier	-ère	épicière
-an	paysan	-anne	paysanne
-en	canadien	-enne	canadienne
-on	lion	-onne	lionne
-f	veuf	-ve	veuve
-x	époux	-se	épouse

B Some other endings are either distinctly masculine or distinctly feminine.

Masculine endings	
-er, -ier	fer, acier
-eau	chapeau
	but not l'eau (*f*), la peau
-et	billet
-c, -d	sac, pied
-ail, -eil	travail, soleil
-oir	soir
-age	fromage
	but not la cage, la page, la rage, l'image, la plage
-ède, ège, -ème	remède, collège, problème
-isme	tourisme
-ment	bâtiment
-ou	genou

Feminine endings	
-ière	bière
	but not le cimetière
-lle	ville
-té, -tte	difficulté, fourchette
-èche, -èque	crèche, bibliothèque
-ffe, -ppe	étoffe, enveloppe
-sse, -nne	caisse, personne
-ace	glace
-aine, -eine, -oine	semaine, reine, macédoine *but not* le moine
-ance, -anse	ambulance, distance
-ence, -ense	essence, défense *but not* le silence
-ure	blessure
-sion, -tion	télévision, question
-ée	l'armée, la journée *but not* le musée, le lycée

exercise

Give the gender (*le, la*) of the following nouns.

a cage *cage*

b problème *problem*

c vendeur *seller*

d glace *ice/mirror*

e semaine *week*

f ambulance *ambulance*

There are a number of French nouns that are identical in spelling and pronunciation, but different in gender and meaning.

A The following list gives examples of nouns whose meanings change according to their gender.

Masculine		Feminine	
l'aide	*male assistant*	l'aide	*help, assistance; female assistant*
le crêpe	*crape fabric*	la crêpe	*pancake*
le critique	*critic*	la critique	*criticism*
le faune	*faun*	la faune	*fauna*
le livre	*book*	la livre	*pound (sterling/weight)*
le manche	*handle (e.g. of broom)*	la manche	*sleeve*
le mémoire	*memorandum; dissertation*	la mémoire	*memory*
le merci	*thanks*	la merci	*mercy*
le mode	*method, way*	la mode	*fashion*
le mort	*dead male*	la mort	*death*
le page	*page(-boy)*	la page	*page (of book)*
le pendule	*pendulum*	la pendule	*clock*
le poêle	*stove*	la poêle	*frying pan*
le poste	*position, job; station (e.g. police); radio / TV set; telephone extension*	la poste	*post (postal service); post office*

le rose	pink (colour)	la rose	rose (flower)
le somme	nap, sleep	la somme	sum, sum total
le tour	(guided) tour; turn; walk; trick	la tour	tower
le vague	vagueness	la vague	wave
le vapeur	steamship	la vapeur	steam, vapour
le vase	vase	la vase	silt, mud
le voile	veil	la voile	sail

B Some anomalies:

Chose *thing* is feminine but **quelque chose** *something* is masculine.

Délice *delight* is masculine in the singular but feminine in the plural.

Personne *person* used as a noun is feminine, but as a pronoun *no one* it is masculine.

exercise

Complete the following sentences with the definite article *le* or *la*.

a Il a cassé _____ vase. *He has broken the vase.*

b Elle a mis les œufs dans _____ poêle. *She put the eggs into the frying pan.*

c Ils ont offert _____ poste à M. Dupont, qui a toujours voulu travailler à _____ poste. *They offered the job to M. Dupont, who has always wanted to work at the post office.*

d Vous avez vu _____ tour Eiffel? *Have you seen the Eiffel Tower?*

Compound nouns are made up of two or more words and fall into categories. Their gender and plurals are governed by certain rules.

Compound nouns can be divided into the following categories.

A Adjective + noun

le grand-père *grandfather* les grands-pères *grandfathers*
la grand-mère *grandmother* les grands-mères *grandmothers*

The gender normally follows that of the noun part. Both parts become plural.

B Noun + noun

le chou-fleur *cauliflower* les choux-fleurs *cauliflowers*
le wagon-lit *sleeper* les wagons-lits *sleepers*

The gender follows that of the main noun, usually the first one. Both nouns become plural.

However, **le timbre-poste** *postage stamp* becomes **les timbres-poste** *postage stamps* in the plural (no -s on the end of **poste**).

C Noun + preposition + noun

l'arc-en-ciel (*nm*) *rainbow* les arcs-en-ciel *rainbows*
le chef-d'œuvre *masterpiece* les chefs-d'œuvre *masterpieces*

With some notable exceptions, the gender is that of the first noun. That noun alone becomes plural. Certain of these nouns remain invariable in the plural, e.g. **le tête-à-tête, les tête-à-tête**.

D Prefix + noun
　la mini-jupe *miniskirt*　les mini-jupes *miniskirts*
The gender is that of the simple noun. The noun alone
becomes plural.

E Adverb + noun
　un haut-parleur *loudspeaker*　les haut-parleurs *loudspeakers*
　un avant-goût *foretaste*　les avant-goûts *foretastes*
The noun alone becomes plural.

F Preposition + noun
　le/la sans-emploi *unemployed person*
　les sans-emploi *unemployed people*
　le sous-titre *subtitle*　les sous-titres *subtitles*
These are usually masculine, unless they refer specifically to a
female person. The plural varies depending on the sense of the
word.

G Verb + noun
　le tire-bouchon *corkscrew*　les tire-bouchon *corkscrews*
　le porte-clefs *keyring*　les porte-clefs *keyrings*
These are usually masculine. The plural is as for preposition +
noun.

H Generally, the plural form is added to noun and adjective
components.

exercise

See exercise 5 in 'More practice'.

Il est and ***c'est*** can both mean *it is*, or *he/she is*, but they are used in different circumstances.

Il and **elle** and their plural forms are used to refer back to specific nouns, as in these examples:

Tu connais Marie? Elle est notaire.	*Do you know Marie?* *She's a lawyer.*
Voici mon ami Paul. Il est canadien.	*Here's my friend Paul.* *He's Canadian.*

In this unit you look at other uses of **il** and the uses of **ce**. (Note that in colloquial speech you may hear **ce** being used instead of **il** in some cases.)

A Il est

• **Il est** + time

Il est sept heures.	*It's seven o'clock.*
Il est tard.	*It's late.*

• **Il est** + adjective + **que**

Il est évident qu'il est intelligent.   *It's clear that he's intelligent.*

• **Il est** + adjective + **de** + infinitive

Il est interdit de marcher sur la pelouse.	*It's forbidden to walk on the grass.*
Il est difficile de juger.	*It's difficult to judge.*

B C'est

• **C'est** + adjective alone, if the reference is to something that has already been mentioned or is otherwise understood

| C'est essentiel. | It's/That's essential. |
| C'est ridicule. | It's/That's ridiculous. |

- **C'est** + noun or pronouns (notice how many ways **ce** can be translated)

C'est Barbara.	It's Barbara.
C'est un fonctionnaire.	He's a civil servant.
C'est un Américain.	He's an American.
C'est mon amie.	She's my friend.
C'est moi.	It's me.
Ce sont mes frères.	They're my brothers.
Qui est-ce?	Who is it?

Although the verb is **sont** when the subject is plural, as in **Ce sont des vélos tout terrain** *They are mountain bikes*, this is not the case with **C'est nous** *It's us* or **C'est eux** *It's them*, etc.

exercise

Complete the following with *c'est*, *ce sont* or *il est*.

E.g. _____ facile? → *C'est* facile.

a _____ vrai que vous êtes malade? Oui, _____ vrai.
Is it true that you're ill? Yes, it's true.

b Quelle heure _____ ? _____ presque midi.
What time is it? It's almost midday.

c _____ vos clés, n'est-ce pas?
These are your keys, aren't they?

d Qui est-ce? _____ mon fils.
Who's that? It's my son.

De combines with the definite article *le*, *la*, *l'* and *les* to produce *du*, *de la*, *de l'* and *des*, meaning *some* or *any*.

A Look at these examples of how French expresses the idea of *some*:

du pain *(some) bread*, de la viande *(some) meat*, des poires *(some) pears*

The word for *some* and *any* varies in French according to the gender and number of the noun that follows it. It is made up of **de** + the definite article and is called the partitive article.

Masculine	de + le → **du**	de + le vin	→ **du vin** *(some/any) wine*
Feminine	de + la → **de la**	de + la confiture	→ **de la confiture** *(some/any) jam*
Masculine and feminine	de + l' → **de l'**	de + l'eau *(nf)*	→ **de l'eau** *(some/any) water*
Plural	de + les → **des**	de + les ordinateurs	→ **des ordinateurs** *(some/any) computers*

B In French the partitive article translates the English *some* and *any*. It is also used when in English neither of these would be used. In all the following cases a form of the partitive article is used in French.

| J'ai de la bière. | *I've got some beer.* |
| Vous avez du vin? | *Have you got any wine?* |

Vous voulez du thé ou du café?	*Would you like tea or coffee?*
Il y a des tomates dans la salade.	*There are tomatoes in the salad.*

C After a negative, **du, de la, de l'** and **des** become **de** when they indicate a lack or an absence of something.

J'ai des enfants.	*I've got children.*
Je n'ai pas d'enfants.	*I don't have any children.*

When no absence or lack is being indicated or a contrast is being made, then the normal form of the partitive article or another article is used:

Je n'ai pas acheté des oranges, j'ai acheté des poires.	*I didn't buy oranges, I bought pears.*
Ce n'est pas un long voyage,	*It's not a long journey.*

exercise

Compile a shopping list of the following items. The gender of each item is given with its illustration.

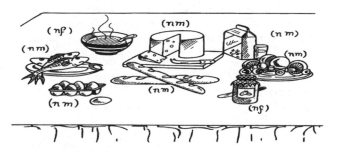

10 simple prepositions (1)

Simple prepositions are single words like *à* (*to* or *at*), *avec* (*with*) or *sans* (*without*)

The following list gives examples of some of the more common prepositions and how they are used. Note the way English and French sometimes use prepositions differently.

A après *after*

Elle est partie après moi.	*She left after me.*

B avant *before (time)*

Il va arriver avant moi.	*He will arrive before me.*
Il a mangé avant de partir.	*He ate before leaving.*

C avec *with*

Jeanne est allée avec Marc.	*Jeanne went with Marc.*
Il mangeait avec son couteau.	*He ate with his knife.*

D chez *to/at the home of, among*

Je vais chez le médecin cet après-midi.	*I'm going to the doctor's this afternoon.*
Je vais rester chez moi ce soir.	*I'm going to stay at home this evening.*
La cuisine est importante chez les Français.	*Cooking is important for the French.*

E contre *against, with*

J'ai laissé mon vélo contre le mur.	*I left my bike against the wall.*

| Vous pouvez échanger cette voiture contre une nouvelle. | *You can exchange this car for a new one.* |
| Il s'est fâché contre elle. | *He got annoyed with her.* |

F dans *on, in, from, until, out of*

• Position

Il est dans le salon.	*He's in the living room.*
J'ai laissé mon journal dans le train.	*I've left my newspaper on the train.*
Elle a pris le café dans le placard.	*She took the coffee of from/out the cupboard.*
Elle buvait dans la boîte.	*She drank from / out of the tin.*

• Time (*after / at the end of which*)

| On se retrouve dans une heure? | *Shall we meet in (after) an hour?* |

exercise

Complete each sentence with an appropriate preposition from the box.

E.g. Je vais _____ Marcel. → Je vais *chez* Marcel.

| contre | avec | chez | après | dans |

a Ils sont arrivés _____ 10 heures.
b Je n'ai rien _____ elle.
c Il a laissé son manteau _____ le train.
d Elle va _____ le dentiste _____ son fils.

The prepositions *depuis*, *derrière*, *devant*, *en*, *entre*, *envers*, *malgré*.

A **depuis** *since, from, for*

Il est là depuis ce matin.	*He's been here since this morning.*
Je travaille ici depuis quatre ans.	*I've worked here for four years.*
Je n'ai pas eu de ses nouvelles depuis des années.	*I haven't had any news from him/her for years.*

B **derrière** *behind*

Le parking se trouve derrière les bureaux.	*The car park is behind the offices.*

C **devant** *in front of, before (location)*

Elle attend devant le cinéma.	*She is waiting in front of the cinema.*
Il passe devant moi.	*He goes before me.*

D **en** *in, by, whilst*

Ils sont en vacances en France.	*They're on holiday in France.*
Il est allé en ville.	*He's gone into town.*
Elle est en ville.	*She's in town.*
Il va à Paris en avion.	*He is going to Paris by plane.*
Ils sont venus en voiture.	*They came by car.*

Note: **à pied** *on foot*, **envoyer par avion** *to send by air*

J'ai fait mes courses en dix minutes.	*I did my shopping in ten minutes.* (i.e *it took me ten minutes*)
Il buvait du café en travaillant.	*He drank coffee whilst working.*
C'était en quelle année? En 1987.	*It was in which year? In 1987.*
Le texte est en espagnol.	*The text is in Spanish.*
Ma chambre est peinte en bleu.	*My room's painted blue.*
Il était en costume.	*He was in a suit.*

E **entre** *between*

Il est entre le cinéma et l'église.	*It's between the cinema and the church.*

F **envers** *towards (with regard to)*

Je n'aime pas son attitude envers moi.	I don't like his attitude towards me.

G **malgré** *in spite of, despite*

Malgré l'heure ils continuaient.	*In spite of the time they went on.*

exercise

See exercise 7 in 'More practice'.

The prepositions *par, parmi, pendant, pour, sans, sous, sur, vers*.

A par *by, in, per*

Ils sont venus par le train.	*They came by train.*
Je l'ai appris par cœur.	*I learnt it by heart.*
L'article a été écrit par un expert.	*The article was written by an expert.*
C'est 5 € par personne.	*It's 5 euros per person.*
On se retrouve deux fois par an.	*We meet twice a year.*
Elle l'a vu par la fenêtre.	*She saw him out of the window.*
Je suis passé par Andorre.	*I went through Andorra.*

B parmi *among*

Vous trouverez des exemples parmi ces chiffres.	*You'll find some examples among these figures.*

C pendant (*during*)

Pendant les vacances j'ai beaucoup lu.	*I read a lot during the holidays.*

D pour *for, in order to*

Ce cadeau est pour toi.	*This present is for you.*
Je suis là pour te voir.	*I'm here to see you.*

E sans *without*

Je ne peux pas le faire sans lui.	*I can't do it without him.*

F sauf *except*

Ils sont tous là sauf elle.   *They're all there except her.*

G sous *under*

Le chat est sous la table.   *The cat's under the table.*

H sur *on, by, in, from, off, over, about*

Les documents sont sur le bureau.   *The documents are on the desk.*

Il a pris la casserole sur la cuisinière.   *He took the saucepan off the cooker.*

La pièce fait cinq mètres sur quatre.   *The room is five metres by four.*

C'est un livre sur la physique.   *It's a book about physics.*

I vers *towards (direction), approximate time*

Il est parti vers Tours.   *He set off towards Tours.*

Je suis parti vers la fin du film.   *I left towards the end of the film.*

exercise

Complete the following using the appropriate preposition.

E.g. Je mange _____ la pause. *during* → Je mange *pendant* la pause.

a Elle a été examinée _____ un spécialiste. *by*

b Votre manteau est _____ les autres sur la chaise. *among*

c La lettre est _____ Mme Dubois. *for*

d Le spectacle commence _____ 22 heures. *at about*

e Je passe mes vacances en France deux fois _____ an. *a/per*

The preposition *de* has a wide range of uses and combines where nescessary with the definite article *le*, *la*, *l'* and *les* to produce *du*, *de la*, *de l'* and *des*.

A possession – expressing *of* or *belonging to* (often *'s* in English):

J'ai perdu la clé de la voiture.	*I've lost the car key.*
Ce sont les vêtements de Michel.	*Those are Michel's clothes.*

B meaning *of* or *from*:

Je voudrais une tasse de thé.	*I'd like a cup of tea.*
Je viens de Belgique.	*I'm from Belgium.*
Je dors de 22 heures à 7 heures.	*I sleep from 10 p.m. until 7 a.m.*
Elle habite à cinq minutes de l'hôpital.	*She lives five minutes from the hospital.*
J'ai besoin d'un feutre.	*I need a felt-tipped pen. (have need of)*

C with measurements:

La pièce fait trois mètres de long.	*The room is three metres long.*

D with certain expressions of time:

Il est six heures du matin.	*It's six o'clock in the morning.*
Il est parti à sept heures du soir.	*He left at seven in the evening.*

E after certain adjectives or **il** + adjective + **de** + infinitive:

Il est facile de réserver une place. *It's easy to reserve a seat.*
Elle était ravie de me voir. *She was delighted to see me.*

F with comparatives **plus** *more* and **moins** *less*, and after a superlative:

Elle gagne plus de 1600 €. *She earns more than 1600 euros.*

C'est le plus grand bâtiment de Paris. *It's the biggest building in Paris.*

G to show the cause of something:

Ils meurent de faim. *They're dying of hunger.*
Il souffre de la grippe. *He's suffering from the flu.*

H with specific verbs

Elle joue du piano. *She's playing the piano.*

exercise

Complete the following using *du, de la, de l', des* or *de*.

E.g. Prenez un verre _____ bière. *Have a glass of beer.* →
Prenez un verre de bière.

a C'est le chat _____ voisin. *It's the neighbour's cat.*
b Il est l'ami _____ Pauline. *He's Pauline's friend.*
c Elle est propriétaire _____ trois cafés. *She's the owner of three cafés.*
d J'ai la brochure _____ hôtel. *I've got the hotel brochure.*
e Ce train va _____ Bruxelles à Paris. *This train goes from Brussels to Paris.*

The preposition *à* can combine with the definite article le, *la*, *l'* or *les* to produce *au*, *à la*, *à l'* and *aux*.

A

Masculine	à + le → au	à + le cinéma → **au cinéma** *at/to the cinema*
Feminine	à + la → **à la**	à + la gare → **à la gare** *at/to the station*
Masculine and feminine	à + l' → **à l'**	à + l'aéroport (*nm*) → **à l'aéroport** *at/to the airport*
Plural	à + les → **aux**	à + les magasins → **aux magasins** *at/to the shops*

B The uses of à:

- location *to, on, in*

Elle va à Paris demain.	*She's going to Paris*
tomorrow.	
J'habite au troisième étage.	*I live on the third floor.*
La photo est à la page 16.	*The photo is on page 16.*
Qu'est-ce qu'il y a à la télé?	*What's on TV?*
Elle est au téléphone.	*She's on the phone.*
J'ai mal à la tête / au dos.	*I've got a headache / back ache.*
Ils habitent au Japon / aux États-Unis.	*They live in Japan / the United States.*

- time (*at, to*)

J'arrive à dix heures.	*I arrive at ten o'clock.*

Nous partons du 3 au 8 mars. *We're away from 3 to 8 March.*

- distance *from*
  Caen se trouve à 40 kilomètres d'ici. *Caen is 40 kilometres from here.*

- transport *by, on*
  Je suis venu à vélo / à bicyclette / à pied. *I came by bike / on foot.*

- description
  Il cherche un homme aux yeux bleus. *He's looking for a man with blue eyes.*
  Je prends un sandwich au fromage. *I'll have a cheese sandwich.*
  Je prends le slip à 6,5 €. *I'll take the briefs that cost 6.5 euros.*

  Ce manteau n'est pas à moi. *This coat isn't mine.*
  Il est facile à ouvrir. *It's easy to open.*

- after certain verbs
  Pierre joue au football. *Pierre's playing football.*

exercise

Give the French for the following, using the vocabulary in brackets.

E.g. *She has a headache.* (la tête) → **Elle a mal à la tête.**

a *His hand is hurting.* (la main)
b *She's got a toothache.* (les dents) (*nfpl*)
c *He's got a bad foot.* (le pied)

Complex prepositions consist of two or more words e.g. *grâce à*. The most commonly used ones include *à* or *de*.

A The following are examples of prepositions that include **à**:

grâce à *thanks to*
par rapport à *with regard to, in relation to*
jusqu'à *up to, as far as, until* quant à *as for*

Je reste ici jusqu'à vendredi. *I'll stay here till Friday.*

As usual when **à** is used with **le, la, l'** and **les**, these words combine and agree with the gender and number of the following word:

Ils sont montés jusqu'au sommet. *They went as far as the summit.*

Allez jusqu'aux feux. *Go up to the traffic lights.*

B The following are examples of prepositions that include **de**:

autour de *around*
à côté de *next to, beside*
en dehors de *outside*
au-dessus de *above*
en face de *opposite*
au milieu de *in the middle of*
en bas de *at the bottom of*
près de *near*

à cause de *because of*
au-delà de *beyond*
au-dessous de *below*
au lieu de *instead of*
en haut de *at the top of*
loin de *far from*
au sujet de *about*

| Il s'est assis à côté de moi. | *He sat down next to me.* |
| Si on sortait au restaurant au lieu de manger à la maison? | *How about going to a restaurant instead of eating at home?* |

As usual when **de** is used with **le, la, l'** and **les**, these words combine and agree with the gender and number of the following word:

| C'est en face du cinéma. | *It's opposite the cinema.* |
| J'habite près de la poste. | *I live near the post office.* |

C The following are examples of complex prepositions that do not end in **à** or **de**:

d'après *according to, in the style of* par-dessus *over*
à travers *through, across* par-dessous *under*

| Son second service est passé juste par-dessus le filet. | *His second service went just over the net.* |

exercise

Match the French with the English.

E.g. en dehors du bâtiment → *outside the building*

a quant à lui
b par-dessus le mur
c en haut de l'arbre
d à travers le terrain de football
e jusqu'à la gare

1 *as far as the station*
2 *as for him*
3 *at the top of the tree*
4 *over the wall*
5 *across the football pitch*

Possessive adjectives indicate possession or a relationship, for example *ma voiture (my car)*, *mon oncle (my uncle)*, *ma tante (my aunt)*.

A The form of the French possessive adjective is determined by the person owning (*my, his, her, our, your, their*) and by the number and, in some cases, the gender of the noun that follows.

B

	Masculine	Feminine	Masculine/Feminine plural
my	mon	ma	mes
your	ton	ta	tes
his/her/ its/one's	son	sa	ses
our	notre		nos
your	votre		vos
their	leur		leurs

C *My:* **mon** is used for masculine nouns, **ma** for feminine nouns, **mes** for all plural nouns. **Mon** is also used before feminine nouns beginning with a vowel (**a, e, i, o, u**) and an unsounded **h**.

(le bureau) mon bureau *my desk* (les dossiers) mes dossiers *my files*

(la veste) ma veste *my jacket* (l'amie) mon amie *my (female) friend*

D *Your*: **ton, ta, tes** are used when referring to someone who is a close friend, a relative or a child. **Ton, ta, tes** behave in the same way as **mon, ma, mes**.

ton stylo	ta maison	tes manteaux
your pen	*your house*	*your coats*

E *His/Her*: **son, sa,** and **ses** each mean *his* or *her* – which one is usually clear from the context. **Son** tells you the gender of **livre**, not the gender of the owner. They behave in the same way as **mon, ma, mes**.

son livre *his/her suit*   ses documents *his/her documents*
sa voiture *his/her car*

F *Our*: **notre** (masculine and feminine singular nouns) and **nos** (plural nouns).

notre fils	notre fille	nos enfants
our son	*our daughter*	*our children*

G *Your*: **votre** (masculine and feminine singular nouns) and **vos** (plural nouns) when referring to someone with whom you are not on familiar terms.

votre ami *your (male) friend*   vos amis *your friends*
votre amie *your (female) friend*

H *Their*: **leur** (masculine and feminine singular) and **leurs** (plural).

leur journal *their newspaper* leurs journaux *their newspapers*

exercise

See exercise 10 in 'More practice'.

In French, adjectives reflect the gender and number of the noun or pronoun they relate to, i.e. masculine or feminine, singular or plural.

A Basic agreement

The basic form of the adjective (as it is found in the dictionary) is used with masculine nouns and pronouns.

Mon ami est espagnol. Il est amusant.	*My friend is Spanish. He's amusing.*

• Most adjectives add an -e when relating to a feminine noun or pronoun.

Mon amie est espagnole.	*My (female) friend is Spanish.*

• When it relates to a plural noun or pronoun the adjective adds an -s.
(Exceptions to this rule are shown in the next unit.)

Mes amis sont espagnols.	*My friends are Spanish.*
Mes amies sont espagnoles.	*My (female) friends are Spanish.*

B Other patterns to note

• Adjectives ending in -e with no accent do not add an extra -e in the feminine form.

jeune *(m)* jeune *(f)* jeunes *(m/fpl)*   *young*

- The following table shows how the feminine endings of various adjectives are formed. You will see that adjectives ending in -n, -l, -s and -t generally double the final consonant in the feminine.

Adjective ending	Masculine	Feminine	
-on	bon	bonne	*good*
	mignon	mignonne	*sweet, pretty*
-en	ancien	ancienne	*ancient, former*
-el	cruel	cruelle	*cruel*
-er	cher	chère	*dear, expensive*
-eil	pareil	pareille	*similar, same*
-as	gras	grasse	*fatty*
-et ⎫ see	net	nette	*clear*
-eur ⎬ Unit	menteur	menteuse	*lying*
-eur ⎭ 18	protecteur	protectrice	*protective*
-f	actif	active	*active*
-g	long	longue	*long*
-c	blanc	blanche	*white*
	public	publique	*public*
	sec	sèche	*dry*

exercise

Look at the following descriptions and choose the correct adjective from the options available.

a Elle a les cheveux court/courts et les yeux verts/vertes.

b Le chien de Jean est méchant/méchante, mais il est aussi timide/timides.

Some adjectives have irregular feminine or plural forms.

A Adjectives ending in **-x** replace the **-x** with **-se** in the feminine, and do not take an **-s** in the masculine plural:

heureux (*m*) heureux (*mpl*) heureuse (*f*) heureuses (*fpl*)
happy

The following are exceptions to this feminine pattern:

doux	doux	douce	douces	*sweet, mild, gentle*
faux	faux	fausse	fausses	*false*

B Adjectives ending in **-s** do not add another **-s** in the masculine plural:

français   français   française   françaises   *French*

C Adjectives ending in **-et** change the ending to **-ète** in the feminine:

secret   secrets   secrète   secrètes   *secret*
also **complet** *full*, **inquiet** *worried*

D A group of adjectives ending in **-eur** add an **-e** in the feminine and do not change the ending to **-euse**:

meilleur   meilleurs   meilleure   meilleures   *better*
also **supérieur** *superior*, **inférieur** *inferior*, **extérieur** *exterior*
and **intérieur** *interior*.

E Adjectives ending in **-al** have irregular masculine plural forms:

normal	normaux	normale	normales	*normal*
BUT				
final	finals	finale	finales	*final*
fatal	fatals	fatale	fatales	*fatal*

F A small group of adjectives have two masculine forms and an irregular feminine form. The second masculine form given below is used before vowels and an unsounded **h**:

le vieux château *the old chateau* le vieil hôtel *the old hotel*

beau/bel	beaux	belle	belles	*beautiful*
fou/fol	fous	folle	folles	*mad*
nouveau/nouvel	nouveaux	nouvelle	nouvelles	*new*
vieux/vieil	vieux	vieille	vieilles	*old*

G The following adjectives are irregular:

bref	brefs	brève	brèves	*brief*
gentil	gentils	gentille	gentilles	*kind*
frais	frais	fraîche	fraîches	*fresh*

exercise

Choose the appropriate form of the adjective in each of these sentences.

E.g. Il possède un très beau/bel cheval. → Il possède un très *beau* cheval.

a C'est la décision final/finale.

b Le vieux/vieil monsieur est très gentil/gentille.

c Est-ce que le lait est frais/fraîche?

d Le nouveau/nouvel hôtel est très beau/belle.

In English adjectives go before the noun they relate to. In French they go before or after.

A The majority of adjectives in French go after the noun.

C'est un livre intéressant.   *It's an interesting book.*

B However, the following commonly used adjectives go before the noun: **autre** *other*; **beau** *beautiful*; **bon** *good*; **court** *short*; **gentil** *kind, nice*; **grand** *big, tall*; **gros** *big, fat*; **haut** *high*; **jeune** *young*; **joli** *pretty*; **long** *long*; **mauvais** *bad*; **même** *same*; **meilleur** *better*; **nouveau** *new*; **petit** *small*; **vieux** *old*.

Ce jeune homme est son fils.   *This young man is his son.*

Ordinal numbers also precede the noun.

Le premier train va à   *The first train goes to*
Cherbourg.   *Cherbourg.*

When used as an adjective, **tout** (**tout, tous, toute, toutes**) stands before the definite article.

Toutes les voitures sont vendues. *All the cars are sold.*

C There are rules to follow when there is more than one adjective with a noun.

• When there are two adjectives they take their normal place before or after the noun.
Un grand arbre mort.   *A big, dead tree.*
Deux bons petits chats.   *Two good little cats.*

• If there is more than one adjective after the noun, they are joined by **et**.

Une femme amusante et intelligente. *An amusing and intelligent woman.*

D **Dernier** and **prochain** have different meanings before and after the noun.

la dernière semaine de l'année	*the last week of the year (i.e. last in a series)*
la semaine dernière	*last week (i.e. the one before this)*
la prochaine réunion	*the next meeting (i.e. next in a series)*
jeudi prochain	*next Thursday (i.e. the one after this)*

When used with a number **dernier** and **prochain** follow the number, unlike English.

les deux derniers mois	*the last two months*
les dix prochaines années	*the next ten years*

exercise

Put the adjective in brackets into the sentence in the correct position, making it agree in number and gender.

E.g. C'est un centre commercial. (nouveau) → C'est un *nouveau* centre commercial.

a J'ai de la bière. (français)
b Il a un ordinateur. (vieux)
c Les documents sont sur ton bureau. (tout, nouveau)
d C'est une histoire. (bon, amusant)

In English adjectives go before the noun they relate to. In French they go before or after.

A Like any adjective, the demonstrative adjective agrees in gender and number with the noun that follows it.

J'aime **ce** journal / **cette** plage. *I like this newspaper / this beach.*

	Singular	Plural
Masculine	ce, cet	ces
Feminine	cette	ces

- **Ce** is used before masculine singular nouns.
  J'ai acheté ce stylo hier. *I bought this/that pen yesterday.*

- **Cette** is used before feminine singular nouns.
  Tu aimes cette table? *Do you like this/that table?*

- **Cet** is used before masculine singular nouns beginning with a vowel or a silent **h**.
  Cet hôtel est excellent. *This/That hotel is excellent.*

- **Ces** is used before masculine and feminine plural nouns.
  Je n'ai plus besoin de ces vêtements. *I don't need these/those clothes any more.*

B If you need to differentiate more clearly between *this* and *that*, or *these* and *those*, -**ci** can be added after the noun to express *this* or *these* (-**ci** comes from **ici** *here*, so it indicates something nearer) and -**là** can be added to express *that* or *those* (**là** means *there*, so it indicates something further away).

Je préfère ce costume-ci.	*I prefer this suit.*
Vraiment? Moi, je préfère ce costume-là.	*Really? I prefer that suit.*
Combien coûte cette chaise-ci?	*How much is this chair?*
Je vais acheter cette chaise-là.	*I'm going to buy that chair.*
Cet hôtel-ci est très bien.	*This (particular) hotel is very good.*
Cet homme-là vend une voiture.	*That man (there) is selling a car.*
Qu'est-ce qu'on prend? Ces fleurs-ci ou ces fleurs-là?	*What shall we buy? These flowers (here) or those flowers (there)?*
Prenons ces fleurs-là.	*Let's take those flowers (there).*

exercise

Match the following with their meanings.

a cette chaise-ci	**1** *that chair*
b ce livre-là	**2** *this chair*
c ces voitures-ci	**3** *those cars*
d ce livre-ci	**4** *that book*
e ces voitures-là	**5** *these cars*
f cette chaise-là	**6** *this book*

An adverb is a word that adds to the meaning of a verb, an adjective or another adverb, for example *carefully*, *loudly*, *mostly*, *extremely*.

In French, most adverbs are formed by adding **-ment** to a form of the adjective.

Elle a simplement refusé.   *She simply refused.*

A For adjectives ending in a consonant the adverb is formed from the feminine form of the adjective. The table below shows a few examples.

Elle parle très doucement.   *She speaks very quietly.*

Masculine adjective	Feminine adjective	Adverb
complet	complète	**complètement** *completely*
franc	franche	**franchement** *frankly*
heureux	heureuse	**heureusement** *happily*

B Adjectives ending in a vowel add **-ment** to the masculine form of the adjective.

Je trouve cela absolument   *I find that absolutely*
 absurde.   *absurd.*

Masculine adjective	Adverb
absolu	**absolument** *absolutely*
facile	**facilement** *easily*
vrai	**vraiment** *truly*

Exceptions to this rule are **fou** *mad*, **gai** *gay, happy* and **nouveau** *new*, which form the adverb from the feminine form of the adjective.

Il se battait follement.   *He struggled madly.*

C Two groups of adverbs are exceptions to the general rules.

• Adjectives ending in -**ant** and -**ent** change the -**nt** to -**mment**.
  Il parle italien couramment.   *He speaks Italian fluently.*

  courant → **couramment** *fluently*   évident → **évidemment** *evidently*

Remember though that **lent** is an exception to this rule and becomes **lentement**.

• A small number of adverbs end in -**ément**, for example:
  commun → **communément** *commonly*

  énorme → **énormément** *hugely*

  précis → **précisément** *precisely*

  profond → **profondément** *profoundly*

exercise

Form adverbs from the following adjectives.

E.g. énorme *enormous* → énormément

a joyeux *joyous*   **d** résolu *resolute*

b vrai *true*   **e** parfait *perfect*

c poli *polite*   **f** profond *profound*

A number of adverbs are very irregular, and some adjectives can be used unchanged as adverbs.

A The adverbs in the table below are irregular.

Il parle brièvement	*He talks briefly.*
Elle écrit bien.	*She writes well.*
Je travaille peu en ce moment.	*I'm not working much at the moment.*
Il court très vite.	*He runs very quickly.*

Masculine adjective	Adverb
bon	**bien** *well*
bref	**brièvement** *briefly*
gentil	**gentiment** *kindly, nicely*
mauvais	**mal** *badly*
meilleur	**mieux** *better*
moindre	**moins** *less*
petit	**peu** *little*

Note: **vite,** meaning *quickly*, has no related adjective; use **rapide** *quick* instead.

B Some adjectives can be used as adverbs in particular expressions or with particular meanings.

bas	*low*	voler bas	*to fly low*
bon	*good*	sentir bon	*to smell good*
mauvais	*bad*	sentir mauvais	*to smell bad*
cher	*expensive*	coûter cher	*to be expensive*

fort	*loudly*	parler fort	*to speak loudly*
juste	*straight, precise*	viser juste	*to aim accurately*
dur	*hard*	travailler dur	*to work hard*
court	*short*	couper court	*to cut short*
clair	*clearly*	voir clair	*to see clearly*
faux	*false*	sonner faux	*to sound wrong*
haut	*loud*	chanter haut	*to sing loudly*
net	*short, clean*	s'arrêter net	*to stop dead*

exercise

Complete each of the following sentences by using a word from the box in its correct form.

E.g. Il est _____ en route. Il est *certainement* en route.

---

bas meilleur mauvais fort net haut bon cher ~~certain~~

---

a Je n'entends rien. Tu parles trop _____ .

b Ces chocolats coûtent _____ .

c Elle travaille _____ que lui.

d Ils parlent _____ le français.

e Ce livre est _____ écrit.

f Le ballon est monté très _____ .

g Ils crient _____ .

h Il s'arrête _____ .

Adverbs can appear in various positions in a sentence. This can depend on the tense of the verb in the sentence.

A In simple tenses (the present, imperfect, future) and in conditional sentences the adverb usually comes straight after the verb it relates to.

Elle parle sérieusement.	*She talks seriously.*
Il travaille lentement.	*He works slowly.*

B Some adverbs may appear at the beginning of a sentence when qualifying the whole phrase. This can be done to give an element of emphasis.

Malheureusement, il était parti.	*Unfortunately, he had gone.*
Demain, elle va à Paris.	*Tomorrow, she's going to Paris.*

C When an adverb qualifies an adjective, the adverb goes first. Where adverbs occur together, **très** *very*, **trop** *too* and **bien** *really, very* go first.

Elle est extrêmement jolie.	*She's extremely pretty.*
Une maison très moderne.	*A very modern house.*
Je le vois trop rarement.	*I see him too rarely.*

D Note that *very much* is **beaucoup**. **Très** can never be used with it.

Il l'a beaucoup aimée.	*He loved her very much.*

E In compound tenses (e.g. the perfect and pluperfect tenses), some shorter adverbs come between the auxiliary verb (**avoir** or **être**) and the past participle.

Il a bien travaillé. *He has worked well.*
Elle l'a vite fait. *She did it quickly.*

assez *enough*	jamais *never*
bien *well*	mal *badly*
beaucoup *a lot*	mieux *better*
bientôt *soon*	moins *less*
déjà *already*	souvent *often*
encore *yet*	toujours *always, still*
enfin *at last*	trop *too much*
vite *quickly*	tout à fait *completely*

F In compound tenses, adverbs of place, some adverbs of time, adverbs ending in -**ment** and other longer adverbs usually follow the past participle.

Je suis arrivé hier. *I arrived yesterday.*
Il a voyagé rapidement. *He travelled quickly.*

aujourd'hui *today*	(avant-)hier *(the day*
demain *tomorrow*	*before) yesterday*
(après-)demain *(the day after)*	autrefois *in former times*
tomorrow	
hier *yesterday* tard *late*	

exercise

See exercise 15 in 'More practice'.

Comparison of adjectives is when you say something is *more … than, (bigger) than, less … than* or *as … as.*

A Simple comparison

• To say *more …* or *(bigg)-er* in French you use **plus** + adjective.

Ce journal est plus sérieux.   *This newspaper is more serious.*

• To say *less …* you use **moins** + adjective.

Ce journal est moins sérieux.   *This newspaper is less serious.*

• To say *(just) as (big)* you use **aussi** + adjective (or **si** in the negative).

Ce garçon est aussi grand.   *This boy is (just) as big.*

Ce garçon n'est pas si/aussi grand.   *This boy isn't as big.*

B Comparing two things

• To say *more … than* or *(bigg)-er than* you use **plus** + adjective + **que**.

Mon frère est plus grand que   *My brother is taller than*
son ami.   *his friend.*

• To say *less (big) than* you use **moins** + adjective + **que**.

Il est moins riche que moi.   *He's less rich than I am.*

• To say *(just) as … as* you use **aussi** + adjective + **que** (or **si … que** in the negative).

Claire est aussi grande que son frère.	*Claire is (just) as tall as her brother.*
Il n'est pas aussi/si riche que moi.	*He's not as rich as me.*

C When used with a noun to indicate quantity (e.g. *more time*, *less wine*) **plus** or **moins** are followed by **de** before the noun.

Il a plus d'argent (que moi).	*He's got more money (than me).*
Elle fait moins de travail (que lui).	*She does less work (than him).*

Note also the similar use of **autant de … que** meaning *as much/many … as*.

Il y a autant de places libres ici que là-bas.	*There are as many free seats here as over there.*

D Some adjectives have irregular comparative forms.

bon *good*	meilleur *better*
mauvais *bad*	pire/plus mauvais *worse*
petit *little*	moindre/plus petit *smaller, lesser*

Plus mauvais refers to quality, **pire** means 'morally worse'.
Plus petit refers to size, **moindre** to significance.

In French you can say **moins bon** *less good* to mean *worse*.

Ce film est moins bon que l'autre.	*This film is worse than the other.*

exercise

See exercises 16 and 17 in 'More practice'.

Comparison of adverbs is when you say does something *more (quickly) than, (faster) than, less (quickly) than* or *as (quickly) as*.

A Simple comparison

- To say *more (quickly)* or *(fast)-er* in French you use **plus** + adverb.

  Il court plus vite.   *He runs faster.*

- To say *less (quickly)* you use **moins** + adverb.

  Il court moins vite.   *He runs less quickly.*

- To say *(just) as (quickly)* you use **aussi** + adverb.

  Ce garçon court aussi vite.   *This boy runs (just) as quickly.*

  Ce garçon ne court pas aussi vite.   *This boy doesn't run as fast.*

B Comparing two things

- To say *more (quickly) than* or *faster than* you use **plus** + adverb + **que**.

  Il écoute plus attentivement que moi.   *He listens more attentively than me.*

- To say *less (quickly) than* you use **moins** + adverb + **que**.

  Anne travaille moins sérieusement que sa sœur.   *Anne works less seriously than her sister.*

- To say *(just) as … as* you use **aussi** + adverb + **que** (or **si … que** in the negative).

Il écoute aussi patiemment que   *He listens (just) as*
    son père.   *patiently as his father.*
Il n'écrit pas aussi/si bien que Pierre.   *He doesn't write as well*
    as Pierre.

To say *as much as* you use **autant que.**
    Cela m'irrite autant que toi.   *That irritates me as much*
    as it does you.

C Some adverbs have irregular comparative forms.
    bien *well*   mieux *better*
    mal *bad*   pis / plus mal *worse*
    peu *little*   moins *less*

    Ce matin on avait des problèmes,   *This morning there were*
        mais maintenant ça va mieux.   *problems but now it's*
        going better.

Note: **Pis** is rarely used except in certain idiomatic expressions:

    Tant pis!   *Too bad!*

exercise

Match the French and English sentences.

a Il court plus vite que moi.   **1** *He speaks more quickly*
    than Sylvie.

b Il parle plus rapidement que Sylvie.   **2** *He runs more slowly*
    than me.

c Il court moins vite que moi.   **3** *He speaks more slowly*
    than Sylvie.

d Il parle moins vite que Sylvie.   **4** *He runs faster than me.*

The fastest, the most expensive are examples of superlative adjectives. They are formed by using the comparative preceded by *le*, *la* or *les*.

A To form the superlative of an adjective you put the definite article (**le**, **la**, or **les**) in front of the simple comparative form.

Cet hôtel est **le plus cher**.	*This hotel is the most expensive.*
Ces hôtels sont **les moins chers**.	*These hotels are the least expensive.*

With two superlative adjectives the definite article is repeated.

Cet hôtel est le plus cher et le plus confortable.	*This hotel is the most expensive and the most comfortable.*

• Both the adjective and the definite article must agree in gender and number with the noun.

le plus **grand** jardin	*the biggest garden*
la région **la** moins **importante**	*the least important region*

• The superlative adjective takes its normal place in relation to the noun.

Sarah est la plus jeune infirmière.	*Sarah's the youngest nurse.*
Sarah est l'infirmière la plus patiente.	*Sarah's the most patient nurse.*

When the adjective comes after the noun the definite article is repeated.

B Superlatives of irregular adjectives

bon	le meilleur	*the best*
mauvais	le plus mauvais / le pire	*the worst*
petit	le moindre	*the least, the slightest*
	le plus petit	*the smallest*

Ce vin est le plus mauvais de tous les vins.	*This wine is the worst of all the wines.*
Ceci est le plus petit sac.	*This is the smallest bag.*
Cela n'a pas la moindre importance.	*That doesn't have the least importance.*

C After the superlative **de** is used to mean *in* or *of*.

C'est l'hôtel le moins cher de la ville.	*It's the cheapest hotel in town.*
Il est le plus doué de tous.	*He's the most gifted of them all.*

D Le **plus ... que**. After this construction the subjunctive is used.

C'est la plus belle région que je connaisse.	*It's the loveliest region I know.*

exercise

See exercise 19 in 'More practice'.

The fastest, the best, etc. are examples of superlative adverbs. They are formed by using the comparative preceded by *le, la* or *les*.

A To form the superlative of an adverb you put the masculine definite article **le** in front of the comparative form. The definite article is invariable; it is always **le**.

Il court le plus vite de tous les athlètes.	*He runs the fastest of all the athletes.*
Elle travaille le moins régulièrement de tous les employés.	*She works the least regularly of all the employees.*
Elle travaille le moins régulièrement et le moins sérieusement de tous les employés.	*She works the least regularly and the least seriously of all the employees.*

With two superlative adverbs **le** has to be repeated.

B The superlative adverb always comes after the verb.

Il mange le plus vite de tous. *He eats the fastest of them all.*

C Superlatives of irregular adverbs

bien	le mieux	*the best*
mal	le plus mal	*the worst*
	le pis	*the worst*
peu	le moins	*the least*

Il tape le moins rapidement. *He types the most slowly.*

D After the superlative, **de** is used to mean *in* or *of*.

Il travaille le plus dur de tous.

He works the hardest of them all.

E In French the expression *as (quickly) as possible* is said with **le plus** + adverb + **possible,** or **aussi** + adverb + **que possible.**

Faites cela, s'il vous plaît, le plus vite possible.

Please do that as quickly as possible.

Faites cela, s'il vous plaît, aussi vite que possible.

Please do that as quickly as possible.

Il a ouvert la porte le plus doucement possible.

He opened the door as quietly as possible.

Il a ouvert la porte aussi doucement que possible.

He opened the door as quietly as possible.

exercise

Complete the sentences using appropriate adverbs from the box.

E.g. Moi, je conduis _____ Pierre, mais toi, tu conduis _____ .
I drive worse than Pierre, but you drive the worst. → Moi, je conduis *pire que* Pierre, mais toi, tu conduis *le plus mal*.

mieux	le plus mal	le mieux	plus mal

a Sophie travaille _____ que Nadine, mais Pascale travaille _____ de tous. *Sophie works better than Nadine, but Pascale works the best of all.*

b Henri chante _____ que Pierre, mais Yves chante _____ de tous. *Henri sings worse than Pierre, but Yves sings worst of all.*

Indefinite adjectives and pronouns include words like *each*, *such*, *other* and *someone*.

The indefinite adjectives and pronouns are as follows:

Adjectives		Pronouns	
aucun(s), aucune(s)	*none, not any*	aucun(s), aucune(s)	*none, not any*
autre(s)	*other*	autre(s)	*other(s)*
certain(s), certaine(s)	*certain*	certain(s), certaine(s)	*certain (ones), some*
même(s)	*same*	même(s)	*same*
tout, tous, toute, toutes	*all*	tout, tous, toute, toutes	*all*
plusieurs	*several*	plusieurs	*several*
		personne	*no one*
chaque	*each*	chacun(e)	*each one*
quelque(s)	*some, a few*	quelqu'un, quelques-uns, quelques-unes	*someone some (people)*
		quelque chose	*something, anything*
tel(s), telle(s)	such		

A number of indefinites have the same form and can be used both as adjectives and pronouns, as shown in the table above.

28 indefinite adjectives and pronouns (1)

- As adjectives

Il arrivera sans **aucun** doute. *He'll arrive without any doubt.*

On prend le **même** bus tous les jours. *We take the same bus every day.*

Nous avons **plusieurs*** pièces à côté. *We have several rooms next door.*

On remet ça à un **autre** jour. *We'll postpone that to another day.*

***plusieurs** does not add an -e in the feminine.

- As pronouns

Je ne vois **aucun** des deux. *I can't see either of them.*

Les **autres** sont au troisième étage. *The others are on the third floor.*

Certains préfèrent travailler ici. *Some prefer to work here.*

Plusieurs des pièces sont délabrées. *Several of the rooms are dilapidated.*

Toutes sont à décorer. *All have to be decorated.*

J'en ai vu **plusieurs**. *I saw several.*

exercise

Complete the following using the appropriate form of the word in brackets.

E.g. Il a préparé (tout) les brochures (*nf*). → Il a préparé toutes les brochures.

a Il y a (plusieurs) voitures (*nf*) à vendre.

b (Tout) les employés (*nm*) sont arrivés.

c J'ai (certain) idées (*nf*) à discuter avec vous.

Some indefinites can only be used as adjectives or pronouns.

A The following indefinites can be used only as adjectives.

chaque	*each*
quelque(s)	*some, a few*
tel(s), telle(s)	*such*

Chaque élève a reçu un stylo. *Each pupil received a pen.*

Quelque temps après, il est arrivé. *Some time later, he arrived.*

Il a fait quelques commentaires. *He made a few comments.*

Cela nous a fait un tel problème! *That caused us such a problem!*

Vous voyez la question telle qu'elle est. *You see the question as it is.*

B The following indefinites can be used only as pronouns.

chacun, chacun(e)	*each one*
personne	*no one*
quelque chose	*something*
quelqu'un	*someone*
quelques-uns, quelques-unes	*some (people)*

• **Chacun, chacune**

Chacun peut prendre un stylo. *Everyone can take a pen.*

• **Personne** can be used on its own or as part of a negative.

Qui est là? Personne. *Who's there? No one.*

Il n'y a personne là. *There's no one there.*

- **Quelque chose**

  J'ai acheté quelque chose au marché.   *I bought something at the market.*

- **Quelqu'un, quelques-un(e)s**

The plural of this is formed with a hyphen.

  Il y a quelqu'un à la porte.   *There's someone at the door.*

  Quelques-uns désirent partir plus tôt.   *Some want to leave earlier.*

exercise

Complete the gaps with an appropriate word from the box, using the English as a guide.

E.g. J'ai perdu _____ . J'ai perdu quelque chose. *I've lost something.*

> chaque   quelque chose   quelqu'un   chacun   personne
> quelques-unes

a _____ a téléphoné. *Someone has telephoned.*

b _____ doit prendre un billet. *Each (one) must take a ticket.*

c Le bureau est vide. _____ n'y travaille. *The office is empty. No one works in there.*

d _____ voyageur porte une valise. *Each traveller is carrying one case.*

e Vous avez des brochures? Oui, j'en ai. *Do you have brochures? Yes, I've got a few.*

f Il reste encore _____ à faire. *There's still something to do.*

Verbs are the part of speech that can change form the most within a sentence.

A Verbs are words that show an *action* or a *state* of affairs and are often called 'doing words'.

B Verbs have a basic form that is called the *infinitive* (in English *to …*). In French the infinitive is indicated by the end of the word: *to carry* = **porter**, *to finish* = **finir**, *to sell* = **vendre**.

C Verbs can be classified into groups. There are two big groups – *regular* verbs and *irregular* verbs. Regular verbs have a common pattern of change (see E below) and are classified into three main types according to the ending of their infinitive: the **-er** verbs, the **-ir** verbs and the **-re** verbs. Irregular verbs each have an individual pattern.

D When a verb is used it has a *subject* which shows who is doing the action. The subject can be a noun or a pronoun: *the women work, he runs*.

E When a verb is shown in its pattern it is shown with the *subject pronouns* (*I, you*, etc.). Changing the infinitive to match its subject is called *conjugating* the verb, for example:

je porte	*I carry*	nous portons	*we carry*
tu portes	*you carry*	vous portez	*you carry*
il porte	*he carries*	ils portent	*they carry*
elle porte	*she carries*	elles portent	*they carry*

F Verbs also change because of their *tense*. Different tenses indicate that an action occurs in the present, in the future or in the past, for example:

present tense	je travaille	*I work, I am working*
future tense	je travaillerai	*I will work*
perfect tense	j'ai travaillé	*I have worked, I worked*
imperfect tense	je travaillais	*I used to work, I was working*

G The perfect tense is an example of a *compound tense*. That means it is made up of two verbs, the *auxiliary* (**ai** above) and the past participle of the *main verb* (**travaillé** above).

H Verbs can be used

• in the *indicative*: the normal everyday use, as those shown in F above
• in the *conditional*: **je préférerais** *I would prefer*
• in the *imperative*: for giving orders or instructions. **Venez ici.** *Come here.*
• in the *subjunctive*: used in French to show, for example, doubt or emotion.

exercise

Match the subject pronouns to the correct part of the verb.

E.g. ils + portent

| 1 nous | 3 tu | **a** portes | **c** portent |
| 2 vous | 4 elles | **b** portons | **d** portez |

A large number of French verbs follow a regular pattern. The largest group are those whose infinitive ends in *-er*.

A To use a regular **-er** verb in the present tense firstly remove the **-er** from the infinitive, which will leave you with the stem of the verb.

travail<u>er</u> *to work* → **travaill-** = stem

You then add the appropriate ending to this stem, as follows.

Singular endings			Plural endings		
I	je	-e	*we*	nous	-ons
you	tu	-es	*you*	vous	-ez
he	il	-e	*they*	ils	-ent
she	elle	-e	*they*	elles	-ent

The pronunciation of the verb is the same for all the endings, apart from the **nous** and **vous** forms.

B Here is an example.

TRAVAILLER *to work*	
je travaille	nous travaillons
tu travailles	vous travaillez
il travaille	ils travaillent
elle travaille	elles travaillent

C Here are some common -er verbs.

aimer *to like, to love*	parler *to speak*
arriver *to arrive*	porter *to carry, to wear*
chanter *to sing*	préparer *to prepare*
chercher *to look for*	regarder *to watch*
écouter *to listen to*	rester *to stay*
fermer *to close*	traverser *to cross*
jouer *to play*	trouver *to find*

D In French there is no equivalent to the English continuous present tense: *I speak* and *I am speaking* are both translated by **je parle**. Here are some more examples.

Elle écoute la radio.	*She listens / She's listening to the radio.*
Nous jouons aux cartes.	*We play / We're playing cards.*
Il cherche son portable.	*He's looking for his mobile phone.*

exercise

Complete the following sentences by filling in the correct verb endings.

E.g. Vous regard_____ la télévision. *You're watching television.* Vous *regardez* la télévision.

a Elle port_____ une jupe. *She's wearing a skirt.*
b Ils écout_____ la radio. *They're listening to the radio.*
c Je prépar_____ le déjeuner. *I'm preparing lunch.*
d Tu cherch_____ quelque chose? *Are you looking for something?*

Some -er verbs have the same endings as regular -er verbs, but the spelling changes slightly in the stem.

A Most verbs ending in -**eter** and -**eler** double the consonant before an unsounded -**e**, that is in all but the **nous** and **vous** forms.

JETER *to throw*		APPELER *to call*	
je je**tt**e	nous jetons	j'appe**ll**e	nous appelons
tu je**tt**es	vous jetez	tu appe**ll**es	vous appelez
il/elle je**tt**e	ils/elles je**tt**ent	il/elle appe**ll**e	ils/elles appe**ll**ent

Similarly **geler** to *freeze*, **peler** to *peel*.

B Some verbs ending in **e** + consonant + **er**, or **é** + consonant + **er** take a grave accent before an unsounded -**e**, that is in all but the **nous** and **vous** forms.

ACHETER *to buy*		ESPÉRER *to hope*	
j'ach**è**te	nous achetons	j'esp**è**re	nous espérons
tu ach**è**tes	vous achetez	tu esp**è**res	vous espérez
il/elle ach**è**te	ils/elles ach**è**tent	il/elle esp**è**re	ils/elles esp**è**rent

Similarly **lever** to *lift, to raise*, **préférer** to *prefer*.

C Verbs ending in -**oyer** or -**uyer** change the **y** to an **i** except in the **nous** and **vous** forms.

ENVOYER *to send*		S'ENNUYER *to be bored*	
j'envoie	nous envoyons	je m'ennuie	nous nous ennuyons
tu envoies	vous envoyez	tu t'ennuies	vous vous ennuyez
il/elle envoie	ils/elles envoient	il/elle s'ennuie	ils/elles s'ennuient

Similarly **employer** *to use*.

The same change occurs but is optional in the present tense of verbs that end in **-ayer** (**payer** *to pay*, **essayer** *to try*).

D -er verbs that end in **-ger** take an -e after the -g- in the **nous** form, and verbs ending in **-cer** change the -c to -ç in the **nous** form. This is in order to retain the soft **g** or **c** sound.

manger *to eat*
commencer *to begin*
nous mangeons *we eat / we are eating*
nous commençons *we begin / we are beginning*

exercise

Fill in the correct part of the missing verb.

E.g. Tu _____ . (jeter) → Tu jettes.

a J' _____ . (appeler)
b Nous _____ dans la mer. (nager)
c Ils _____ de dormir. (essayer)
d Tu _____ souvent des spaghettis? (manger)
e Elle _____ des cadeaux. (acheter)

A large number of French verbs follow a regular pattern. One group are those whose infinitive ends in -*ir*.

A To use a regular -**ir** verb in the present tense remove the -**ir** from the infinitive, which will leave you with the stem of the verb.

rempl<u>ir</u> *to fill* → **rempl**- = stem

You then add the appropriate ending to this stem as follows.

Singular endings			Plural endings		
I	je	-is	*we*	nous	-issons
you	tu	-is	*you*	vous	-issez
he	il	-it	*they*	ils	-issent
she	elle	-it	*they*	elles	-issent

The **je, tu, il** and **elle** forms are pronounced in the same way: the final -**s** and -**t** are not pronounced.

B Here is an example.

FINIR *to finish*	
je finis	nous finissons
tu finis	vous finissez
il finit	ils finissent
elle finit	elles finissent

C Here are some common -**ir** verbs.

applaudir *to applaud, to clap*   grandir *to grow*
choisir *to choose*   maigrir *to lose weight*

obéir *to obey*   réussir *to succeed*
réfléchir *to think about* rougir *to blush*

D There are a small number of -**ir** verbs that take the endings of -**er** verbs in the present tense.

OUVRIR *to open*	
j'ouvre	nous ouvrons
tu ouvres	vous ouvrez
il ouvre	ils ouvrent
elle ouvre	elles ouvrent

Other verbs in this group include **offrir** *to offer*, **souffrir** *to suffer* and **cueillir** *to pick, to gather*.

exercise 1

Replace the infinitive in brackets with the correct form of the verb.

E.g. Je (rougir) *I blush*. → Je rougis.

a Il (obéir) *He obeys.*
b Ils (applaudir) *They are clapping.*
c Nous (réussir) *We are succeeding.*
d Elle (finir) *She finishes.*
e Vous (ouvrir) *You open.*
f Elles (souffrir) *They are suffering.*

exercise 2

Translate the following into French.

a *She is opening the present.*
b *He chooses a pen.*
c *Everyone applauds.*
d *They fill the bottles.*

A third category of verbs end in -re in the infinitive, and many follow a common pattern.

A To use an **-re** verb in the present tense remove the **-re** from the infinitive, which will leave you with the stem of the verb.

vendre *to sell* → **vend-** = stem

You then add the appropriate ending to this stem as follows.

Singular endings			Plural endings		
I	je	-s	*we*	nous	-ons
you	tu	-s	*you*	vous	-iez
he	il	–	*they*	ils	-ent
she	elle	–	*they*	elles	-ent

You will notice that the latter half of the verb (plural endings) follows the same pattern as regular -er verbs.

Pronunciation of the **je**, **tu**, **il** and **elle** forms is the same. Although the **-ent** ending isn't pronounced, for **ils** and **elles** it does cause the preceding consonant to be pronounced (e.g. in **ils vendent** you pronounce the **d**).

B Here is an example.

PERDRE *to lose*	
je perds	nous perdons
tu perds	vous perdez
il perd	ils perdent
elle perd	elles perdent

C Further examples of -re verbs that follow this pattern in the present tense are:

vendre *to sell*	fondre *to melt*
attendre *to wait (for)*	entendre *to hear*
répondre *to reply, to answer*	rendre *to give back, to*
descendre *to descend, to*	*return*
go *down*	correspondre *to*
	correspond

Je vends des voitures.	*I sell cars.*
Tu attends le bus, Michel?	*Are you waiting for the bus, Michel?*
Il répond à la question.	*He replies to the question.*
Nous descendons maintenant.	*We are coming down now.*
Ils rendent l'argent.	*They return the money.*
Elles entendent un bruit.	*They hear a noise.*

exercise

Insert the correct form of the verb into the gap provided.

E.g. il _____ , vous _____ (rendre) → **il rend, vous rendez**

a j' _____ , ils _____ (attendre)

b vous _____ , elle _____ (vendre)

c tu _____ , elles _____ (entendre)

d ils _____ , nous _____ (perdre)

e nous _____ , il _____ (descendre)

Reflexive verbs express an action that reflects back to the subject. Their infinitives incluse the reflexive pronoun *se*.

A Reflexive verbs are recognizable in the infinitive by the reflexive pronoun **se**. They can be **-er**, **-ir**, or **-re** verbs and are conjugated in the same way as other verbs. The reflexive pronoun **se** changes according to the subject.

Common reflexive verbs include **s'amuser** *to enjoy oneself*, **se promener** *to go for a walk*, **s'appeler** *to be called*, **se doucher** *to shower*, **se raser** *to shave*, **s'arrêter** *to stop*, **s'habiller** *to get dressed*, **se reposer** *to rest*, **se coucher** *to go to bed*, **se lever** *to get up*, **se réveiller** *to wake up*.

B Here is an example of a reflexive verb, showing conjugation and all the reflexive pronouns.

SE LAVER *to wash (oneself)*	
je **me** lave	nous **nous** lavons
tu **me** laves	vous **vous** lavez
il/elle **se** lave	ils/elles **se** lavent

C Reflexive verbs are also used to describe action to parts of the body.

Je me brosse les dents.	*I brush my teeth.*
Elle se casse la jambe.	*She breaks her leg.*

D Two common reflexive verbs are **se passer** *to happen* and **se trouver** *to be situated.*

Qu'est-ce qui se passe?	*What is happening?*
Le village se trouve au sud de Paris.	*The village is south of Paris.*

E A number of verbs that are not normally reflexive can be used reflexively to include the meaning *each other, oneself, themselves,* or *to each other.*

Je me demande où il est?	*I wonder (ask myself) where he is?*
Ils se téléphonent chaque jour.	*They telephone each other every day.*

When used in such cases with **on** meaning *we*, the reflexive pronoun **se** means *(to) ourselves* or *(to) each other / one another.*

On s'écrit souvent.	*We often write to each other.*

Non-reflexive verbs can be used reflexively where in English we might use a passive to say how things are done, or how they happen, or how they are.

Ça s'écrit avec un S.	*It's written/spelt with an S.*
Ça se dit.	*It's said like that. / You hear that.*
Ce vin se boit avec le poisson.	*This wine is drunk with fish.*

exercise

Unscramble the following sentences.

E.g. douche matin je me le. *I shower in the morning.* → Je me douche le matin.

a il à lève se heures sept. *He gets up at seven o'clock.*

b les brossent elles dents se. *They brush their teeth.*

c nous à heures couchons nous onze. *We go to bed at eleven o'clock.*

d les me cheveux lave je. *I wash my hair.*

Subject pronouns can stand in place of a noun to indicate who is performing the action of a verb. They are words such as *I*, *you*, *he*, *she*, etc.

A

Singular	Grammatical name	Plural	Grammatical name
je *I*	first-person singular	nous *we*	first-person plural
tu *you*	second-person singular	vous *you*	second-person plural
il *he, it*	third-person singular	ils *they*	third-person plural
elle *she, it*	third-person singular	elles *they*	third-person plural
on *one (they)*	third-person singular		

B The subject pronoun goes before the verb in a statement (or in a statement used as a question), or after the verb in a question. **Je** becomes **j'** before a vowel.

J'apprends le français.	*I'm learning French.*
Allez-vous en France cette année?	*Are you going to France this year?*
Elle ne va pas au musée.	*She's not going to the museum.*

C The second-person singular, **tu**, is familiar and used when addressing people you are close to, children and pets. **Vous** is formal and is used with all other individuals. **Vous** is also used when addressing more than one person, whether you know them closely or not.

D Il, elle, ils and elles are used for both people and things and mean *he*, *she*, *it* and *they*. These must always be the same in number and gender as the noun they are referring to.

Paul? Il est ici. Anne? Elle est là-bas. — *Paul? He's here. Anne? She's over there.*

Cette église? Elle est très vieille. — *This church? It's very old.*

Les poires? Elles sont dans la cuisine. — *The pears? They're in the kitchen.*

E Several masculine nouns together, or several feminine nouns together, are referred to by the appropriate gender of pronoun in the plural.

Paul et Henri, où sont-ils? — *Where are Paul and Henri?*

Ghislaine et Marie, où sont-elles? — *Where are Ghislaine and Marie?*

When a mixed group of males and females, or of masculine and feminine objects, are referred to together with one pronoun, that pronoun is masculine plural.

Paul et Ghislaine, où sont-ils? — *Where are Paul and Ghislaine?*

La cathédrale et le château, ils datent du 15ème siècle. — *The cathedral and the château date from the 15th century.*

exercise

See exercise 26 in 'More practice'.

The subject pronoun *on* is used frequently in French. It refers to an unspecified person or people and is generally translated by *one*, *people*, *someone*, *we* or *they*.

On can refer to one person or several, its meaning depending on the context in which it is used. It is always used with the third-person singular part of the verb.

On m'a dit qu'il pleut.	*Someone told me it's raining.*
On se retrouve au cinéma?	*Shall we meet at the cinema?*

A **On** can mean *one*, non-specific *you*, *they* or *people*.

En général on va en vacances en été.	*People usually go on holiday in summer.*
On mange quand on a faim.	*You eat when you are hungry. / One eats when one is hungry.*
On ne sait jamais.	*You never know. / One never knows.*
En France on boit du vin pendant le repas.	*In France they drink wine with meals.*

B **On** can mean *someone* or non-specific *they*, and is often used in French when a passive form is used in English.

On m'a donné un plan de la ville.	*Someone gave me / I was given a town map.*
On va demander une pièce d'identité.	*Someone / They will ask / You'll be asked for a means of identification.*

On m'a dit que tu étais au théâtre hier soir.	*Someone told me / I was told you were at the theatre last night.*

C In informal French **on** is often used to mean *we* instead of **nous**.

On t'a vu au théâtre hier soir.	*We saw you at the theatre last night.*
Qu'est-ce qu'on va faire?	*What shall we do?*
On va en ville?	*Shall we go to town?*

- When **on** replaces **nous**, any adjective used is usually in the plural, although the verb remains in the singular.

Nous sommes fatigués.	*We are tired.*
On est fatigués.	*We are tired.*

- In compound tenses with **être** the past participle can be singular or plural.

On est rentré(-s/-es) à minuit.	*We came home at midnight.*
On est arrivé(-s/-es) trop tard.	*We arrived too late.*

exercise

Translate the following using *on*.

a *We're going to France at Easter.*
b *We eat at eight.*
c *Shall we meet tomorrow?*
d *Sometimes we prefer the cinema to the theatre.*

Emphatic pronouns are usally used for emphasis or after a preposition, as in the examples *I don't know, It's me!, Go with him*.

A Here is a full list of emphatic pronouns.

Singular		Plural	
moi	*me*	nous	*us*
toi	*you*	vous	*you*
lui	*him*	eux	*them*
elle	*her*	elles	*them*
soi	*oneself*		

B These pronouns are often used for emphasis of the subject or object.

Moi, j'aime voyager en voiture.	*I like travelling by car.*
Tu m'énerves, toi!	*You get on my nerves, you do!*

C They are also used with **c'est** or **ce sont** (in any tense) and with **qui** and **que**.

C'est moi.	*It's me.*
C'est moi qui vais en ville.	*I'm the one who's going into town.*
C'est elle que je vois régulièrement.	*She's the one I see regularly.*

D They can be used in answer to a question and after **pas**.

Qui a-t-elle rencontré? Lui! *Who did she meet? Him!*

Qui veut faire la vaisselle? Pas moi! *Who wants to wash up?*
Not me!

E Emphatic pronouns are used after prepositions, including:
après *after*, **avant** *before*, **avec** *with*, **chez** *at the home of*,
derrière *behind*, **devant** *in front of*, **pour** *for*, **sans** *without*,
vers *towards*.

chez moi *at my place, at home*   derrière lui *behind him*

They are used after the preposition **à** to show possession.

Cette veste est à moi. *This jacket is mine.*

F After **comme**.

Elle travaille à Paris comme moi. *She works in Paris like*
me.

G With comparisons.

Il court plus vite que moi. *He runs faster than me.*

H With a double subject or object.

Mon mari et moi y seront. *My husband and I will*
be there.

exercise

Translate the following into French.

a *I prefer red wine.*

b *He works here, not me.*

c *Her? She's got a headache.*

d *Me, I'm going with them.*

Possessive pronouns are words such as *mine, yours, his, hers* and *theirs*, which stand in place of a possessive adjective + noun.

A The form of the possessive pronoun, like the possessive adjective (**mon, ma, mes,** etc.) is determined by the person owning (*mine, yours*, etc.) and by the gender and number of the noun it stands for.

> Tu peux me prêter ton journal?　*Can you lend me your*
> J'ai oublié le mien.　　　　　　*newspaper? I've forgotten*
> 　　　　　　　　　　　　　　　 *mine.*

	Masculine singular	Feminine singular	Masculine plural	Feminine plural
mine	le mien	la mienne	les miens	les miennes
yours	le tien	la tienne	les tiens	les tiennes
his/hers/its/one's	le sien	la sienne	les siens	les siennes
ours	le nôtre	la nôtre	les nôtres	
yours	le vôtre	la vôtre	les vôtres	
theirs	le leur	la leur	les leurs	

> Merci bien. Ça c'est ma　　　 *Thank you very much. That's*
> tasse, à côté de la sienne. (*i.e.*　*my cup next to his/hers.*
> *feminine singular for* tasse)
> Voici un stylo. C'est le tien? (*i.e.*　*Here's a pen. Is it yours?*
> *masculine singular for* stylo)

J'ai mes papiers. Vous avez les vôtres? (*i.e. masculine plural for* papiers) *I've got my papers. Have you got yours?*

B The definite article (**le, la, les**) is an integral part of the possessive pronoun. When occurring with **à** or **de** it combines with them in the usual way.

J'aime bien ta robe – je la préfère à la mienne. *I like your dress – I prefer it to mine.*

Votre bureau est à côté du mien. *Your office is next to mine.*

Nos chambres sont en face des leurs. *Our rooms are opposite theirs.*

C **À** + an emphatic pronoun (**moi, toi,** etc.) is used to indicate who something belongs to.

Cette photo est à qui? Elle est à moi/nous. *Whose is this photo? It's mine/ours.*

À qui est ce foulard? C'est à elle. *Whose is this scarf? It's hers.*

exercise

Replace the phrase in italics with an appropriate possessive pronoun.

E.g. Il a son journal et *mon journal.* → Il a son journal et le mien.

a Ce sont mes gants. Où sont *tes gants*?
b Paul va chercher ses clés et *mes clés*.
c Nous avons nos passeports. Avez-vous *vos passeports*?

40 demonstrative pronouns

Demonstrative pronouns replace a demonstrative adjective + noun, and mean *the one(s)*, *this/that one* and *these/those*.

A Celui, celle, ceux, celles

The form of the demonstrative pronoun changes according to the gender and number of the noun it relates to.

	Singular	Plural
Masculine	celui	ceux
Feminine	celle	celles

- When followed by **qui**, **que** or **dont**, the demonstrative pronouns mean *the one(s) that*, or, when referring to people, *the one(s) / he / she / those who*.

  Celui qui parle est mon frère. *The one who's speaking is my brother.*

  Je n'aime pas ces chaussures. Je *I don't like these shoes.*
  préfère celles que vous avez là-bas. *I prefer the ones you have over there.*

- When followed by **de**, demonstrative pronouns can indicate possession.

  Ce n'est pas ma raquette, c'est *It's not my racket, it's*
  celle de mon père. *my father's.*

- The suffixes **-ci** (for *this, these*) and **-là** (for *that, those*) can be added in order to reinforce the contrast between *this/that one*, *these/those (ones)*.

  celui-ci, celle-ci *this (one)*   ceux-ci, celles-ci *these (ones)* celui-là, celle-là *that (one)* ceux-là, celles-là *those (ones)*

Quel journal prenez-vous? Je *Which newspaper will you*
prends celui-ci/celui-là. *have? I'll take this one /*
that one.

B Ceci (*this*) and cela (*that*)

These do not refer to a specific noun that has been mentioned, but to an idea, event, fact or object. Cela is frequently shortened to ça in speech. Ça and cela are the most commonly used forms, and are both often used to mean *this* as well as *that*. Ceci is less common.

Je n'aime pas cela/ça. *I don't like that.*
Ça suffit. *That's enough.*

C Ce means *it* and *that*, and is mainly used with the verb être.

C'est mon ami. *It's/That's my friend.*
Ce n'est pas juste. *That's not fair.*

exercise

Follow the example to answer the questions below.

E.g. C'est votre bureau? (patron (*nm*)) Non, c'est celui de mon patron.

a C'est ton stylo? (sœur)

b Ce sont vos papiers? (collègue (*nm*))

c C'est ta veste? (père (*nm*))

Qui* means *who, which,* or *that*. *Que* means *whom, which,* or *that*.

Qui and que and other relative pronouns introduce relative clauses. Both qui and que can refer to people and things. Qui is the subject of the verb that follows, whereas que is the object of the verb that follows.

La voiture **qui** est en panne est une Peugeot.	*The car that's broken down is a Peugeot.*
La voiture **que** vous voulez acheter est trop chère.	*The car that you want to buy is too expensive.*
Les brochures **qui** ont gagné le prix du meilleur dessin sont arrivées.	*The brochures that won the design award have arrived.*
Les brochures **que** nous avons préparées sont arrivées.	*The brochures that we prepared have arrived.*

A Qui is the *subject* of the following verb and means *who/that* for people and *which/that* for things.

Voici Alex, **qui** habite chez nous.   *Here's Alex, who lives with us.*

In this sentence qui is the subject of the verb habite.

Le paquet **qui** est arrivé est pour toi.   *The parcel that has arrived is for you.*

In this sentence qui is the subject of the verb est arrivé.

B Que is the *direct object* of the following verb and means *who(m)/that* for people and *which/that* for things. It is abbreviated to qu' before a vowel or unsounded h.

| Le garçon que vous avez rencontré est mon fils. | *The boy (whom/that) you met is my son.* |

Que refers to **le garçon** and is the object of the verb **avez rencontré**. (The subject of the verb **avez rencontré** is **vous**.)

| La table qu'il a réservée* est pour quatre personnes. | *The table (that) he reserved is for four people.* |

Que refers to **la table** and is the object of **a réservée**. (The subject of the verb **a réservée** is **il**.)

*A past participle following **que** agrees in gender and number with the word that **que** refers to.

Unlike its English equivalents, **que** can never be omitted in French.

exercise

Choose the appropriate relative pronoun in each sentence.

E.g. C'est la femme qui/que est la patronne du café. → C'est la femme qui est la patronne du café. *It's the woman who runs the café.*

a Il a la clé que/qui tu cherches. *He's got the key that you are looking for.*

b Elle parle des documents que/qui sont dans mon bureau. *She's talking about the documents that are in my office.*

c Le client que/qui vient demain s'appelle Laclos. *The client who is coming tomorrow is called Laclos.*

Dont means *of which, of whom* or *whose*. **Où** means *where* or *when*.

A **Dont** is used for both people and things.

• It can mean *of whom, of which*. It may be used with a verb + **de** (**parler de** *to speak about*, **avoir besoin de** *to need, have need of* or with an adjectival phrase + **de** (**être fier de** *to be proud of*).

Voici le livre dont j'ai besoin.	*Here's the book (that) I need.* (lit. *of which I have need*)
L'hôtel dont j'ai parlé est au coin.	*The hotel (that) I spoke about is on the corner.*
Voici le prix dont il est si fier.	*Here's the prize (that) he's so proud of.*

• It can indicate possession and mean *whose*.

J'ai rencontré un client dont j'ai oublié le nom. (J'ai oublié le nom **du** client.)	*I met a customer whose name I have forgotten.*
J'ai rencontré Michelle, dont tu m'as présenté le père. (le père **de** Michelle)	*I met Michelle, whose father you introduced to me.*

While in English you can sometimes leave out the relative pronoun, **dont** can never be omitted in French.

B **Où** generally means *where*.

Le parc où jouent les enfants va fermer.
The park where the children play is going to close.

- It can also replace a preposition + **lequel**.

La boîte où (= dans laquelle) vous trouverez les livres est dans le salon.
The box you'll find the books in (in which you'll find…) is in the sitting room.

- It is used to mean *when* after **le jour**, **le mois**, etc.

Il pleuvait le jour où tu es arrivé.
It was raining on the day (when) you arrived.

Les autres sont arrivés au moment où je partais.
The others arrived at the moment when / just as I was leaving.

C **Dont** cannot be used after a preposition – **lequel** etc. must be used instead.

C'est un joli lac, **au milieu duquel** il y a une petite île.
It's a pretty lake, in the middle of which there's a little island.

exercise

See exercise 32 in 'More practice'.

Lequel, laquelle, lesquels and *lesquelles* are relative pronouns and are used after a preposition to mean *whom, that* or *which*.

A The relative pronoun **lequel** agrees in gender and number with the noun it relates to, and has the following forms.

	Singular	Plural
Masculine	lequel	lesquels
Feminine	laquelle	lesquelles

These pronouns are used with prepositions to introduce a relative clause.

C'est la société pour laquelle je travaille.

It's the company I work for (for which I work).

B When used with the preposition **à**, or a complex preposition ending in **à**, the two combine to form **auquel, à laquelle, auxquels, auxquelles**. These replace à + noun. When referring to a person, **à qui** can also be used.

Le cinéma auquel il est allé est à dix minutes d'ici.

The cinema he's gone to (to which he has gone) is ten minutes from here.

Le client auquel/à qui j'ai donné les papiers est dans votre bureau.

The client I gave the papers to (to whom I gave…) is in your office.

C When used with the preposition **de**, or a complex preposition ending in **de**, the two combine to form **duquel, de**

laquelle, desquels, desquelles. These replace de + noun. For people, de qui and dont are preferred.

| Les résultats à propos desquels vous m'avez écrit sont inquiétants. | *The results you wrote to me about (about which…) are worrying.* |
| Les personnes dont / de qui on parlait n'étaient pas présentes. | *The people (who(m)) we were talking about weren't there.* |

D After **parmi** and **entre**, only **lequel** and its forms can be used; **qui** is not used.

| Nous avons 15 employés, parmi lesquels 8 sont des diplômés. | *We have 15 employees, of whom 8 have a higher qualification.* |

Qui is used, however, with other prepositions when referring to people, as well as with **à** and **de** (above).

| La femme avec qui je travaille est très gentille. | *The woman I work with is very kind.* |

exercise

Choose the correct form of the relative pronoun.

E.g. C'est l'agence avec lequel/laquelle il a négocié. *It's the agency he negotiated with.* → C'est l'agence avec laquelle il a négocié.

a Voici la femme avec lequel/laquelle j'ai dansé. *Here's the woman I danced with.*

b Ce sont les amies auxquels/auxquelles j'ai envoyé la carte. *These are the friends I sent the card to.*

44 relative pronouns (4)

Ce qui and *ce que* both mean *what* or *which*, in the sense of *that which* or *the thing which*. *Ce dont* means *of which*.

A **Ce qui** is the subject of the verb that follows.

Je ne sais pas ce qui se passe.	*I don't know what is happening.*

Ce qui is the subject of the verb **se passe**.

Elle n'est pas encore arrivée, ce qui est bizarre.	*She's not arrived yet, which is strange.*

Notice that here **ce qui** is the subject of **est bizarre** and refers back to a whole clause (**elle n'est pas encore arrivée**).

B **Ce que** (**ce qu'** before a vowel or unsounded **h**) is the object of the verb that follows.

Je ne sais pas ce qu'il va faire.	*I don't know what he is going to do.*

Ce que is the object of the verb (**va**) **faire**.

Elle n'est pas retournée, ce que je ne comprends pas.	*She has not returned, which I don't understand.*

Ce que is the object of the verb **comprends** and refers back to the whole clause.

C **Ce dont** is the indirect object of the verb that follows.

• **parler de** *to speak of* or *about*

Ce dont il parle est grave.	*What he's talking about is serious. (The thing of/about which he's talking)*

- **avoir besoin de** to need (have need of)

Il est malade. Je sais ce dont il a besoin.

He's ill. I know what he needs (has need of).

- **avoir peur de** to be afraid of

Il a perdu son emploi. C'est ce dont il avait peur.

He's lost his job. That's what he was afraid of (the thing of which he was afraid).

D **Tout ce qui, tout ce que/qu'** and **tout ce dont** mean *all / everything / that / which / of which.*

Tout ce qu'il y a dans la valise est à moi.

Everything in the suitcase is mine.

C'est tout ce qu'il a dit.

That's all he said.

exercise

Tout ce qui or tout ce que/ce qu'?

E.g. Il fait _____ il veut. *He does everything he wants.* → Il fait tout ce qu'il veut.

a Prenez _____ vous voulez. *Take everything you want.*

b Comprenez-vous _____ se passe? *Do you understand all that's happening?*

c Je vais vous montrer _____ il y a. *I'll show you everything there is.*

d J'ai compris _____ il a dit. *I understood everything he said.*

e Il est parti avec _____ il possédait. *He left with everything he owned.*

There are three types of object pronouns – direct object pronouns, indirect object pronouns and y and en.

A The direct object of a verb can be replaced by a direct object pronoun:

Vous prenez **la chambre**?	*Will you take **the room**?*
Oui, je **la** prends.	*Yes, I'll take **it**.*

and the indirect object can be replaced by an indirect object pronoun:

Vous allez parler **à ce client**?	*Are you going to talk **to this customer**?*
Oui, je **lui** parle cet après-midi.	*Yes, I'm talking **to him** this afternoon.*

B The form of these pronouns shows the gender and number of the object.

Me, te, le and **la** become **m'**, **t'** and **l'** before a vowel or unsounded **h**.

	Direct object	Indirect object	
je	me	me	*(to) me*
tu	te	te	*(to) you*
il	le	lui	*(to) him/it*
elle	la	lui	*(to) her/it*
nous	nous	nous	*(to) us*
vous	vous	vous	*(to) you*
ils	les	leur	*(to) them*
elles	les	leur	*(to) them*

C The object pronoun can also have an abstract sense, in which case it is always masculine. In this usage there is not always an equivalent in English.

Je **le** sais. *I know (it).*   Je **l'**espère. *I hope so.*

D Use of the direct object pronoun

Pourquoi est-ce que tu **me** regardes?	*Why are you looking at* **me**?
Il **la** retrouve une fois par semaine.	*He meets **her** once a week.*
Elle **vous** admire beaucoup.	*She admires **you** very much.*

E Use of the indirect object pronoun

Il **me** dit bonjour chaque matin.	*He says hello **to me** every morning.*
Je **leur** écris deux fois par mois.	*I write **to them** twice a month.*

In the imperative the indirect object pronouns **me** and **te** change to **moi** and **toi**.

Donnez-les-**moi**.   *Give them to me.*

exercise

See exercise 35 in 'More practice'.

The pronoun *y* often means *(to) it, (to) them* or *(to) there*. *En* replaces *de* + noun and translates into English as *some, of it* or *of them*.

A Y stands for **à** (or another preposition) + noun and generally means *there, to there, it* or *to it*.

Vont-ils au théâtre? Oui, ils y vont à sept heures.	*Are they going to the theatre? Yes, they're going (there) at 7 o'clock.*
Tu connais Biarritz? Oui, j'y ai passé mes vacances.	*Do you know Biarritz? Yes, I spent my holiday there.*

Remember, where the English may leave out the word *there* the French never omits **y**.

• In verb constructions with **à** (e.g. **penser à**), y can replace **à** + noun.

Le problème? J'y pense beaucoup.	*The problem? I think about it a lot.*

But **y** cannot be used to refer to a person. An indirect object pronoun or a preposition with an emphatic pronoun must be used instead.

À Jeanne? Oui, je lui ai répondu.	*Jeanne? Yes, I've replied to her.*

B En replaces **de** + noun and translates into English in a number of ways. Like **y**, **en** can never be omitted.

Son article? Il en est très fier.	*His article? He's very proud of it.*

Tu connais Paris? Oui, j'en reviens justement. *Do you know Paris? Yes indeed, I've just come back (from there).*

• **En** replaces a partitive article + noun.

Vous voulez du café? Oui, j'en veux bien merci. *Would you like some coffee? Yes, I would like some please.*

• It replaces **de** + noun (or a simple noun) in expressions of quantity.

Elle a trois kilos de tomates. J'en ai quatre. *She's got three kilos of tomatoes. I've got four (of them).*

• It is used with verbs and expressions using **de** such as **avoir besoin de** (*to need*), **se souvenir de** (*to remember*), **parler de** (*to talk about*).

Villandry? Je m'en souviens bien. *Villandry? I remember it well.*

But when referring to people **en** is not always used (except in answer to **combien?**).

Jean et de Christine? Oui, je me souviens bien d'eux. *Jean and Christine? Yes, I remember them well.*

Combien de frères a-t-il? Il en a deux. *How many brothers has he got? He's got two (of them).*

exercise

See exercise 36 in 'More practice'.

Object pronoun position varies with the type of verb structure.

A In all tenses, the object pronoun goes before the conjugated verb. In compound tenses this is the auxiliary verb.

Elle **les** aide dans la cuisine.	*She is helping them in the kitchen.*
Elle **lui** téléphonait souvent.	*She used to telephone him frequently.*
Il **l'**a acheté hier.	*He bought it yesterday.*
Elle **leur** avait donné les cadeaux.	*She had given them the presents.*

This position is the same in questions, whichever question form is used.

Le prenez-vous?	*Are you taking it?*
Est-ce qu'il **l'**a acheté hier?	*Did he buy it yesterday?*

B With **aller** + infinitive, and with verbs such as **vouloir** and **pouvoir** + infinitive, the pronoun goes before the verb it relates to.

Je vais **lui** parler demain.	*I'll talk to him tomorrow.*
Tu peux **l'**ouvrir maintenant.	*You can open it now.*

C Where there is more than one pronoun the order is as follows:

Il **me le** promet pour demain.	*He's promised it to me for tomorrow.*
Elle **les leur** offre comme cadeau.	*She's giving them to them as a gift.*

SUBJECT	1	2	3	4	5	VERB
	me					
	te	le	lui	y	en	
	se	la				
	nous	les	leur			
	vous					

D In affirmative imperatives, object pronouns come after the verb and are joined to it with a hyphen. Where there are two or more pronouns the direct object precedes the indirect object. **Me** and **te** become **moi** and **toi**.

Achetez-**le-moi**. *Buy it for me.*   Prends-**en**. *Take some.*

In negative imperatives, object pronouns precede the verb and **moi** and **toi** revert to **me** and **te**. The pronouns appear in the normal order.

Ne **me le** donnez pas.   *Don't give it to me.*
Ne **les lui** donne pas.   *Don't give them to him/her.*

exercise

See exercises 37 and 38 in 'More practice'.

Avoir (to have) is an irregular verb. Its pattern is unlike that of any other verb.

A The present tense of **avoir** *to have* is formed as shown.

AVOIR *to have*	
j'ai *I have*	nous avons *we have*
tu as *you have*	vous avez *you have*
il a *he/it has*	ils ont *they have*
elle a *she/it has*	elles ont *they have*

B In many cases **avoir** is used in French in much the same way as the verb *to have* is used in English.

J'ai deux enfants.	*I have two children.*
Tu as des passe-temps?	*Do you have any hobbies?*
Elle a un frère.	*She has a brother.*
Vous avez des sœurs?	*Do you have any sisters?*
Ils ont un nouveau patron.	*They've got a new boss.*

C There are some expressions in French that use **avoir** when in English you would use the verb *to be*. This is because the French expressions use a noun, not an adjective.

Quel âge avez-vous?	*How old are you?*
J'ai 24 ans.	*I'm 24.*

Similarly:

avoir chaud	*to be hot*	j'ai chaud	*I'm hot*
avoir froid	*to be cold*	j'ai froid	*I'm cold*
avoir raison	*to be right*	j'ai raison	*I'm right*

avoir tort	*to be wrong*	j'ai tort	*I'm wrong*
avoir faim	*to be hungry*	j'ai faim	*I'm hungry*
avoir soif	*to be thirsty*	j'ai soif	*I'm thirsty*
avoir peur	*to be afraid*	j'ai peur	*I'm afraid*
avoir de la chance	*to be lucky*	j'ai de la chance	*I'm lucky*
avoir sommeil	*to be tired/ sleepy*	j'ai sommeil	*I'm tired/sleepy*
avoir honte	*to be ashamed*	j'ai honte	*I'm ashamed*

exercise

Use the words from both boxes to translate the sentences shown below.

E.g. Il a + faim. *He's hungry.*

Tu as	Il a	Nous avons	J'ai	Elle a	Ils ont	Vous avez	Elles ont

peur	faim	tort	de la chance	une maison secondaire
	trois filles	un rendez-vous	une nouvelle voiture	

a *You're wrong.*
b *He's afraid.*
c *You've got a new car.*
d *I'm hungry.*

e *They're lucky.*
f *She's got an appointment.*
g *They've got three daughters.*
h *We've got a second home.*

Être (to be) is an irregular verb. Its pattern is unlike that of any other verb.

A The present tense of **être** *to be* is formed as shown.

ÊTRE *to be*	
je suis *I am*	nous sommes *we are*
tu es *you are*	vous êtes *you are*
il est *he/it is*	ils sont *they are*
elle est *she/it is*	elles sont *they are*

B In many cases **être** is used in French in much the same way as the verb *to be* is used in English.

Je suis marié(e).	*I'm married.*
Il est célibataire.	*He's single.*
Vous êtes occupé(e)?	*Are you busy?*
Elles sont canadiennes.	*They're Canadian.*
Ils sont en France.	*They're in France.*

Être is not used for saying your age, nor for a number of expressions in which *to be* is used in English. Many use **avoir** instead.

J'ai cinq ans. *I'm five years old.*

There is a list of these expressions in Unit 48.

C **Être** is used to say what job someone does. The noun is then used without any article (unless there's an adjective or other qualifier).

Elle est ingénieur.	*She's an engineer.*
Vous êtes comptable?	*Are you an accountant?*
C'est un bon médecin.	*He's a good doctor.*
C'est une professeur expérimentéee.	*She's an experienced teacher.*

D In English, the continuous present tense uses the verb *to be* plus another verb ending in *-ing*, for example *He is washing the car (is* from *to be,* plus *washing)*. In French only one verb is used to express this: **Il lave la voiture.**

exercise 1

Complete the sentences with the appropriate personal subject pronouns.

E.g. _____ êtes anglais? *Vous* êtes anglais?

a _____ suis très heureux!   d _____ est fou!

b _____ sont au théâtre.   e _____ es très gentil.

c _____ sommes allemands.

exercise 2

Être or *avoir*? **Translate the following into English.**

a *He's 10.*   e *You're right.*

b *I'm an engineer.*   f *She's happy.*

c *I'm hungry.*   g *Are you thirsty?*

d *They're Spanish.*   h *She's pretty.*

Aller (to go) and *faire (to make* or *do)* are two common irregular verbs.

ALLER *to go* (present tense)	
je vais	nous allons
tu vas	vous allez
il/elle va	ils/elles vont

FAIRE *to make/to do* (present tense)	
je fais	nous faisons
tu fais	vous faites
il/elle fait	ils/elles font

A • **Aller** means *to go*.

Ils vont à la piscine.   *They are going to the swimming pool.*

• **Aller** can also be used to say how people are.

Comment allez-vous? *How are you?*   Je vais bien/mieux. *I'm well/better.*

Comment ça va? *How are things?*   Ça va bien/mal. *They're fine / not good.*

• **Aller** can also be used to say what someone is going to do, usually in the near future. In this case it is always followed by an infinitive.

Elles vont jouer au tennis.   *They're going to play tennis.*

Il va se lever.   *He's going to get up.*

B • **Faire** means *to make* or *to do*.

Elle fait un gâteau.   *She's making a cake.*

Ils font toujours leurs devoirs.   *They always do their homework.*

- **Faire** is also used in impersonal constructions to talk about the weather.

Il fait beau. *It's fine.*
Il fait chaud. *It's hot.*
Il fait du soleil. *It's sunny.*
Il fait froid. *It's cold.*

Il fait du brouillard. *It's foggy.*
Il fait du vent. *It's windy.*

- It is used for sports in the combination **faire + du / de l' / de la + noun.**

Elle fait de la natation.   *She's swimming / She swims.*

Also: **faire du football** to *play football*, **faire du ski** to *ski*, **faire du vélo** to *go cycling*, **faire de la voile** to *sail*, etc.

- **Faire** also describes other activities, in the combination **faire + noun.**

Il fait la lessive.   *He's doing the washing.*

Also: **faire la vaisselle** to *do the washing-up*, **faire la cuisine** to *cook*, etc.

- And it is used with money or measurements.

Ça fait 15 €.   *That's 15 euros (comes to 15 euros).*

La pièce fait 3 mètres sur 2.   *The room measures 3 metres by 2.*

exercise

See exercises 39 and 40 in 'More practice'.

Mettre (to put) and **prendre (to take)** are both irregular verbs.

METTRE *to put* (present tense)	
je mets	nous mettons
tu mets	vous mettez
il/elle met	ils/elles mettent

PRENDRE *to take* (present tense)	
je prends	nous prenons
tu prends	vous prenez
il/elle prend	ils/elles prennent

Compounds of these verbs follow the same pattern (e.g. **promettre** *to promise*, **comprendre** *to understand*.)

A Mettre is used in the following ways:

• to mean *to put*
Il met les livres à l'étagère.   *He puts the books on the shelf.*

• to mean *to put on* (clothes, etc.)
Elle met ses lunettes / son manteau.   *She puts on her glasses / her coat.*

• to mean *to switch on*
Il met la radio.   *He switches on the radio.*

• with an expression of time, to indicate time spent
Je mets une heure à faire mes courses.   *I take / It takes me an hour to do my shopping.*

• when reflexive, it means *to begin, to start*
Ils se mettent à marcher très tôt.   *They start to walk very early.*

B **Prendre** is used in the following ways:

- to mean *to take*, and also *to have / to take* (food, drink or when shopping, etc.)

  Elle prend son sac.   *She takes her bag with her.*
  Je prends un café.   *I'll have a coffee.*
  Il prend ses médicaments.   *He takes his medicine.*
  Je prends un kilo de pommes.   *I'll have/take a kilo of apples.*

- to mean *to catch*, *to take*, *to get* (transport) and *to take / to have* (a shower or bath)

  Il prend le train à 10 heures.   *He's catching the train at 10 o'clock.*

  Il prend une douche.   *He's having a shower.*

- to mean *to take / to last* with expressions of time (when used impersonally)

  Ça prend une heure.   *It takes an hour.*

BUT

  Je mets une heure à le faire.   *I take an hour to do it.* (see **mettre** above)

exercise

Translate the following into French.

a *Are you learning English?*
b *I'm going to have a cup of tea.*
c *She's having a shower.*
d *He promises a good dinner.*
e *I'm going to put my coat on.*

Two common irregular verbs are *pouvoir* and *vouloir*. They are usually followed by an infinitive and are known as modal verbs.

POUVOIR *to be able to* (present tense)	
je peux	nous pouvons
tu peux	vous pouvez
il/elle peut	ils/elles peuvent

VOULOIR *to wish, want* (present tense)	
je veux	nous voulons
tu veux	vous voulez
il/elle veut	ils/elles veulent

A **Pouvoir** is mainly used with the infinitive of another verb. It indicates:

- ability

Je ne peux pas me lever.	*I can't get up.*

- permission

Vous pouvez partir si vous voulez.	*You can/may go if you like.*
Je peux regarder le film avec vous?	*Can I watch the film with you?*

- possibility

Il peut avoir dix ans.	*He could be ten years old.*

When translating verbs of perception or sensation (*to hear*, *to see*, *to understand*, etc.) **pouvoir** is not used in French and the verb of sensation stands alone.

J'entends les voisins.	*I can hear the neighbours.*
Je ne vois pas très bien.	*I can't see very well.*

B **Vouloir** is used to indicate:

- a desire or wish (followed by an infinitive or a noun)

Je veux acheter un pullover.	*I want to buy a pullover.*
Tu veux un verre de vin?	*Do you want a glass of wine?*

- an intention or willingness

  Je veux rentrer à six heures. *I want (intend) to go home at six.*

- a wish (in this case it is sometimes used in the conditional and can be used with another verb or a noun).

Je voudrais une omelette.	*I'd like an omelette.*
Il voudrait vous accompagner.	*He'd like to go with you.*
Je voudrais bien y aller.	*I'd really like to go.*

- a polite request

  Voulez-vous attendre un moment? *Please wait a moment.*

exercise

Translate the following ito French.

a *She wants to go to the bank.*
b *You can eat now.*
c *He wants to buy a bike.*
d *I would like a kilo of apples.*
e *We can go in now.*

Devoir and *savoir* are irregular verbs. They can be followed by an infinitive and, in this case, are known as modal verbs.

DEVOIR *to have to (must)* (present tense)	
je dois	nous devons
tu dois	vous devez
il/elle doit	ils/elles doivent

SAVOIR *to know* (present tense)	
je sais	nous savons
tu sais	vous savez
il/elle sait	ils/elles savent

A **Devoir** is used to indicate

- an obligation or necessity (translating *must, have to*)

Il doit prendre le train de dix heures.	*He has to catch the ten o'clock train.*
Vous devez aller la voir.	*You must go and see her.*
Tu dois attendre une heure.	*You('ll) have to wait an hour.*

- a probability or supposition

Elle doit être en retard.	*She must be late.*

- an intention (meaning *meant to / supposed to*)

Le car doit partir à onze heures.	*The coach should / is meant to / is supposed to leave at eleven o'clock.*

- *should* or *ought to*, when used in the conditional

Vous devriez partir bientôt.	*You should leave soon.*

Devoir also means *to owe* (usually used with a noun).
    Elle lui doit 200 €   *She owes him 200 euros.*

B Savoir means

• *to be able to (know how to)* when referring to skills
    Elle sait nager.   *She can (knows how to) swim.*

Note: **Pouvoir** is used for permission or ability in specific circumstances.

    Il peut nager ici/aujourd'hui.   *He can swim here/today.*

• *to know* when talking about facts or information
    Il est déjà parti. Oui, je le sais.   *He's already left. Yes, I know.*

    Je sais qu'il va arriver à 7 heures.   *I know that he's arriving at 7 o'clock.*

Note: **Connaître** *to know, to be acquainted with* must be used if you are talking about knowing people or places.
    Je connais la ville de Nancy.   *I know the town of Nancy.*

exercise

Translate the following into French.

a *I must go to Paris.*
b *He must be in the living room.*
c *She must ring Rouen.*
d *We know how to ski.*
e *They must promise.*
f *I know Saumur well.*

There are rules that govern the form of the verb when it has more than one subject (*My friend and I are...*).

A Using the **nous** (first-person plural) form of the verb:
The **nous** form of the verb is appropriate when the two or more people who make up the subject of the verb include you.

Ma sœur et moi (= nous) **travaillons** ensemble.	*My sister and I work together.*
Mes amis et moi (= nous) **sortons** aujourd'hui.	*My friends and I are going out today.*

In such cases the third-person singular subject pronoun **on** is often used to sum up two subjects, and means *we*.

Julie et moi, on part ensemble.	*Julie and I are going away together.*

B Using the **vous** (second-person plural) form of the verb:
The **vous** form of the verb is used when the two or more people who make up the subject of the verb include the person you are talking to (but do not include you). This applies whether you are on **tu** or **vous** terms with the person you are speaking to.

Vous et vos amis (= vous) **pouvez** venir avec nous.	*You and your friends can come with us.*
Louise et toi (= vous) **êtes** arrivés samedi?	*Did you and Louise arrive on Saturday?*

C Using the **ils/elles** (third-person plural) form of the verb:
The **ils/elles** form of the verb is the appropriate choice when the two or more people who make up the subject of the verb do not include either you or the person you are talking to.

M. et Mme Durand (= ils) **regardent** un film.	M. *and Mme Durand are watching a film.*
Pierre et ses amis (= ils) **sont** allés à la gare.	Pierre *and his friends have gone to the station.*
Mme Grand et Mlle Duplessis (= elles) **travaillent** ensemble.	Mme Grand *and Mlle Duplessis work together.*

exercise

Complete the gaps with the *nous* or the *ils/elles* form of the verb given in brackets.

E.g. Jean et Luc _____ au football. (jouer) Jean et Luc *jouent* au football.

a M et Mme Leclerc _____ acheter une nouvelle voiture. (vouloir) *M and Mme Leclerc want to buy a new car.*

b Mon collègue et moi _____ prendre le train. (devoir) *My colleague and I must catch the train.*

c Pierre et moi _____ toujours le dimanche après-midi. (se promener) *Pierre and I always go for a walk on Sunday afternoon.*

d Mon frère et ses amis _____ aller à Paris. (vouloir) *My brother and his friends want to go to Paris.*

In English, the present participle is the part of the verb that ends in *-ing*, as in the sentence *She left the room singing*.

A The French present participle is formed by taking the **nous** form of the present tense, removing the **-ons** and adding **-ant**.

(nous prenons) pren + ant → **prenant** *taking*

B The spelling change to the stem of verbs ending in **-ger** and **-cer** is maintained.

(nous mangeons) **mangeant** (nous commençons) **commençant**

C There are three irregular present participles.

(avoir) **ayant** (être) **étant** (savoir) **sachant**
having *being* *knowing*

D The present participle is used alone to describe circumstances, a situation or a sequence.

Étant malade, je ne suis pas allé. *Being ill I didn't go.*
Il est parti, prenant avec lui *He left, taking all he needed*
  tout ce dont il avait besoin. *with him.*

E It is used with **en** to convey

• the idea of simultaneity (in English *while, whilst, on, in, when … -ing*):

En montant dans le bus, j'ai *(While) getting on the bus,*
  laissé tomber mon sac. *I dropped my bag.*

The fact of two things happening together can be reinforced by using **tout en**:

Tout en écrivant, il m'a répondu. *He answered me whilst*
                                 still writing.

• the manner or method of doing something (in English *by -ing*):

Je me suis occupé en lisant. *I kept myself busy by reading.*

F The French present participle is used to translate some English verbs of action.

Elle est entrée en courant. *She ran in (came running in).*

G The present participle can be used as an adjective, and then agrees in number and gender with the noun it refers to. It can also be used as a noun, and as such also shows number and gender.

Elle est amusante. *She's amusing.* Ils sont amusants. *They're amusing.*

un passant *passer-by (male)* une passante *passer-by (female)*

However, the English *-ing* is sometimes rendered differently in French:

Nous aimons faire du vélo. *We like cycling.*

Il est parti sans dire au revoir. *He left without saying goodbye.*

exercise

See exercise 43 in 'More practice'.

The imperative is used to give instructions and orders, to make requests or to offer suggestions.

A In French there are three forms of the imperative: the **tu**, the **nous** and the **vous** forms.

• The **tu** form comes from the **tu** part of the present tense, with **tu** omitted.

Tu prends un taxi. } → Prends un taxi.
You take a taxi. } → *Take a taxi.*

The exceptions to this rule are all -er verbs, including **aller**. For these, you remove the -s from the **tu** part of the present tense:

Oui, chante. *Yes, sing.* Va chez le médecin. *Go to the doctor's.*

When the imperative is followed by the pronouns **y** and **en**, this -s is retained for reasons of pronunciation.

Vas-y! *Go on!*   Manges-en.   *Eat some.*

• The **nous** form is the **nous** part of the present tense, with **nous** omitted.

Regardons un film.   *Let's watch a film.*

• The **vous** form is the **vous** part of the present tense, with **vous** omitted.

Achetez du pain.   *Buy some bread.*

B The imperative forms of **avoir**, **être** and **savoir** are irregular.

Sois gentille avec ta sœur.   *Be nice to your sister.*
Ayez de la patience.   *Be patient.*

	ÊTRE	AVOIR	SAVOIR
(tu)	sois	aie	sache
(nous)	soyons	ayons	sachons
(vous)	soyez	ayez	sachez

C In the negative, **ne … pas** enclose the imperative and any object pronouns.

Ne riez pas! *Don't laugh!* Ne l'ouvrez pas. *Don't open it.*

D Reflexive verbs

- In the affirmative the reflexive pronoun is placed after the verb and joined to it by a hyphen and **te** is replaced by **toi**: **Tais-toi!** *Be quiet!* **Dépêchez-vous!** *Hurry up!*

- However in the negative the pronoun reverts to its normal form and position: **Ne te dépêche pas.** *Don't hurry.*

exercise

Complete the following instructions, using both *tu* and *vous*:

E.g. (Fermer) la porte. → Ferme la porte. Fermez la porte.

a (Aller) aux magasins. *Go to the shops.*

b N'(avoir) pas peur. *Don't be afraid.*

c (Mettre) du sucre dans le café. *Put some sugar in the coffee.*

d (Prendre) cette rue-là. *Take that road.*

Infinitives are often used after another verb. They can be the subject of a clause.

Infinitives are frequently used after a finite verb. In such cases any negative is formed by putting **ne ... pas** either side of the first verb (or its auxiliary), or both before the infinitive if this is being negated. An infinitive can appear:

A after verbs expressing liking and disliking, e.g. **aimer** *to like, to love,* **adorer** *to adore,* **détester** *to detest, to hate* and **préférer** *to prefer*:

    Je n'aime pas chanter.   *I don't like singing.*
    Nous préférons aller au théâtre.   *We prefer to go to the theatre.*

B after verbs expressing wishing and willing, e.g. **désirer** *to desire,* **espérer** *to hope* and **souhaiter** *to wish*:

    Elle souhaite visiter le château.   *She wants to visit the castle.*
    J'espère ne pas y aller.   *I hope not to go.*

C after verbs expressing perception, e.g. **écouter** *to listen to,* **entendre** *to hear,* **regarder** *to watch,* **sentir** *to feel, to smell,* **voir** *to see* and **sembler** *to appear*:

    Je le vois arriver chaque matin.   *I see him arrive every morning.*

D after verbs expressing motion, e.g. **aller** *to go,* **entrer** *to enter,* **descendre** *to do down, to descend,* **monter** *to go up, to* *ascend*, **rentrer** *to return, to go home*, **sortir** *to go out*, **venir** *to come*:

Venez prendre un café avec moi.	*Come and have a coffee with me.*
Il rentre faire ses devoirs.	*He's going home to do his homework.*

E after the modal verbs **devoir** *to have to*, **pouvoir** *to be able to*, **savoir** *to know how to*, **vouloir** *to want to*:

Elle ne sait pas nager.	*She can't swim.*
Vous pouvez commencer.	*You can begin.*

F after the verbs **falloir** *to be necessary*, **laisser** *to let, to permit* and **faire** *to do, to make*:

Il faut payer.	*We must pay.*
Je laisse Pierre regarder le film.	*I'm letting Pierre watch the film.*
Je me suis fait couper les cheveux.	*I had my hair cut.*

G The infinitive can be used as the subject of a clause.

Décider n'est pas toujours facile.	*Deciding is not always easy.*

exercise

How would you say that you...

E.g. ... *wish to go on holiday in June?* → Je souhaite aller en vacances en juin.

a ... *like swimming?*   **c** ... *must pay?*

b ... *prefer reading?*   **d** ... *want to go to bed?*

The infinitive can be used after prepositions, interrogatives, certain adjectives and, in some circumstances, after nouns, pronouns and adverbs.

A Infinitives are used after simple and complex prepositions and after interrogatives (e.g. **après**, **par**, **pour**, **sans**, **avant de**, **au lieu de**; **comment**, **quand**, **que**, **où**, **combien**, etc.)

Il a commencé par ouvrir la lettre.	*He began by opening the letter.*
Pour aller à la gare, s'il vous plaît?	*How do I get to the station, please?*
Avant de partir elle leur a téléphoné.	*Before leaving she telephoned them.*
Comment savoir qu'il était là?	*How were we to know he was here?*
Que faire dans ces circonstances?	*What's to be done in the circumstances?*

Also after a verb + **à** (e.g. **aider à** *to help*, **apprendre à** *to learn to*, **commencer à** *to start*, **se décider à** *to decide*, **hésiter à** *to hesitate*, **inviter à** *to invite*).

Elle a réussi à préparer le repas.	*She managed to get the meal ready.*
Il hésite à acheter la voiture.	*He's hesitating about buying the car.*

And after a verb + **de** (e.g. **cesser de** *to stop, to cease*, **décider de** *to decide*, **conseiller de** *to advise*, **essayer de** *to try*, **finir de** *to finish*, **oublier de** *to forget*).

A-t-il cessé de pleuvoir? *Has it stopped raining?*
J'ai essayé de trouver le numéro. *I've tried to find the number.*

B Infinitives are used after an adjective + à (e.g. **facile à** *easy to*, **(im)possible à** *(im)possible to*, **intéressant à** *interesting to*, **prêt à** *ready to*).

Vous êtes tous prêts à partir? *Are you all ready to leave?*
Ce plat est très facile à cuisiner. *This dish is very easy to cook.*

And after an adjective + de (e.g. **capable de** *capable of*, **certain de** *certain to*, **content de** *happy to*, **désolé de** *sad/unhappy to*, **heureux de** *happy to*, **sûr de** *sure to*, **surpris de** *surprised to*, **triste de** *sad to*).

Elle est certaine de gagner. *She is certain to win.*

Infinitives are also used after a noun, pronoun, or adverb + à/de.

Quel plaisir de vous revoir! *What a pleasure to see you again!*

J'ai un nouveau bureau à visiter. *I've got a new office to look at.*

Je n'ai rien à vous dire. *I've nothing to say to you.*
Il y a trop à faire. *There's too much to do.*

exercise

See exercise 44 in 'More practice'.

Some French verb constructions require direct objects or indirect objects, while in English the pattern can be different.

A Some verbs take a direct object in French but in English have a preposition after them.

J'attends Pierre en bas.	*I'll wait for Pierre downstairs.*
J'ai payé le repas.	*I've paid for the meal.*

attendre *to wait for* **chercher** *to look for* **demander** *to ask for* **écouter** *to listen to* **regarder** *to look at* **payer** *to pay for*

B Some verbs take an indirect object with **de** in French, but a direct object in English.

Je me souviens bien de Cannes. *I remember Cannes well.*

avoir besoin de *to need* **(se) changer de** *to change* **jouer de** *to play (an instrument)* **manquer de** *to lack, to miss* **se souvenir de** *to remember*

C Some verbs take an indirect object with **à** in French, but a direct object in English.

Je vais répondre à Daniel bientôt. *I'll answer Daniel soon.*

jouer à *to play (a sport)* **(dés)obéir à** *to (dis)obey* **répondre à** *to answer* **ressembler à** *to look like* **téléphoner à** *to telephone*

D Some verbs take two objects: a direct and an indirect object.

Il donne un vélo à son fils.	*He gives his son a bike / a bike to his son.*

donner quelque chose à quelqu'un	*to give something to someone*
vendre quelque chose à quelqu'un	*to sell something to someone*
prêter quelque chose à quelqu'un	*to lend something to someone*

This group includes verbs expressing *taking away* with **à**: **acheter/demander/emprunter/prendre/voler quelque chose à quelqu'un.**

| Il m'a emprunté un stylo. | *He borrowed a pen from me.* |

E The English construction *to ask someone to do something* is translated into French in two principal ways:

• verb + direct object + **à** + infinitive

| Elle a encouragé Paul à participer. | *She encouraged Paul to participate.* |
| Il l'a invitée à manger. | *He invited her to eat.* |

• verb + indirect object + **de** + infinitive

Pierre a demandé à Anne de venir.	*Pierre asked Anne to come.*
Je leur ai dit de ne pas venir demain.	*I told them not to come tomorrow.*
Elle m'a conseillé de rester.	*She advised me to stay.*

exercise

See exercise 45 in 'More practice'.

The perfect is a compound tense required when you want to refer to a completed action in the past: *I went, he has bought*.

A This tense has two parts and is formed from:
- the present tense of the verb **avoir** or, for a small number of verbs, **être**; this is called the auxiliary verb;
- the past participle of another verb, normally formed from the stem of the verb + -é for -er verbs (**manger** → **mangé**); -i for -ir verbs (**finir** → **fini**); -u for -re verbs (**vendre** → **vendu**).

ACHETER (+ AVOIR)		ALLER (+ ÊTRE)	
j'ai acheté	*I bought / have bought*	je suis allé(e)	*I went / have been*
tu as acheté	*you bought / have bought*	tu es allé(e)	*you went / have been*
il a acheté	*he bought / has bought*	il est allé	*he went / has been*
elle a acheté	*she bought / has bought*	elle est allée	*she went / has been*
nous avons acheté	*we bought / have bought*	nous sommes allé(e)s	*you went / have been*
vous avez acheté	*you bought / have bought*	vous êtes allé(e)(s)(es)	*you went / have been*
ils ont acheté	*they bought / have bought*	ils sont allés	*they went / have been*
elles ont acheté	*they bought / have bought*	elles sont allées	*they went / have been*

B Irregular past participles
Some past participles are irregular. A few examples are given here.

avoir → eu	être → été	faire → fait
devoir → dû	dire → dit	mettre → mis

pouvoir → pu	savoir → su	vouloir → voulu
prendre → pris	venir → venu	

C Examples:

J'ai trouvé un billet de vingt euros.	*I found / have found a twenty euro note.*
Elles ont vendu leur maison.	*They sold / have sold their house.*
A-t-il acheté la voiture?	*Did he buy / Has he bought the car?*
Nous n'avons pas encore mangé.	*We haven't eaten yet.*

exercise

Insert the appropriate past participles from the box into the
postcard. The first one has been done for you.

Nous nous amusons bien ici à Paris!

Ce matin, nous avons (a) visité le musée du Louvre et
j'ai (b)...un déjeuner superbe! J'ai beaucoup
(c)...la Joconde. Cet après-midi, nous avons
(d)...des cadeaux et des souvenirs, et tu ne vas pas
le croire - j'ai (e)...Jacques et Valérie dans une librairie!

À très bientôt,

Hélène

acheté	~~visité~~	rencontré	mangé	aimé

The perfect tense is used when referring to a completed action in the past. Some verbs take *être* as their auxiliary.

A There are 14 verbs (plus their compounds and all the reflexive verbs) that use **être** to form the perfect tense. They include regular and irregular verbs. Most indicate motion or a change of state, and to some extent they form pairs.

Infinitive	Past participle	Infinitive	Past participle
aller *to go*	allé	descendre *to go down*	descendu
venir *to come*	venu	monter *to go up*	monté
arriver *to arrive*	arrivé	tomber *to fall*	tombé
partir *to leave*	parti	mourir *to die*	mort
rester *to stay*	resté	naître *to be born*	né
entrer *to go in*	entré	retourner *to return*	retourné
sortir *to go out*	sorti	rentrer *to come/go home*	rentré

B The past participle of these verbs agrees in number and gender with the subject of the verb.

Elle est sortie avec ses amies.   *She's gone out with her friends.*

VENIR *to come*	
je suis venu(e)	nous sommes venu(e)s
tu es venu(e)	vous êtes venu(e)(s)(es)
il/elle est venu(e)	ils/elles sont venu(e)s

Note: With **on** agreement is optional: **On est allé(e)(s)(es).** *We went.*

C Some of the above verbs can be used transitively, that is, with an object. When this is the case they are conjugated with **avoir**.

	with **être**	with **avoir**
descendre	Je suis descendu(e).	J'ai descendu l'escalier.
	I went downstairs.	*I went down the stairs.*
monter	Je suis monté(e).	J'ai monté ma valise dans ma chambre.
	I went up(stairs).	*I took my case up to my room.*
retourner	Je suis retourné(e) à la gare.	J'ai retourné le tableau.
	I went back to the station.	*I turned the painting over.*
sortir	Je suis sorti(e) hier soir.	J'ai sorti l'argent de ma poche.
	I went out last night.	*I took the money from my pocket.*
rentrer	Je suis rentré(e) à minuit.	J'ai rentré la voiture.
	I came home at midnight.	*I have put the car away.*

exercise

Translate the following sentences into French.

a *She came out of the station.*
b *They came out of the cinema.*
c *She fell off the bike.*
d *He went into the bank.*
e *She was born on 4 January.*

There are important points to remember concerning past participle agreement when reflexive verbs are used in the perfect and other compound tenses.

A All reflexive verbs use **être** rather than **avoir** to form the perfect tense. As with all other verbs that use **être**, the past participle must agree with the subject of the verb.

SE LEVER (*to get up, to stand up*)	
je me suis levé(e)	nous nous sommes levé(e)s
tu t'es levé(e)	vous vous êtes levé(e)(s)(es)
il s'est levé	ils se sont levés
elle s'est levée	elles se sont levées

Je me suis réveillé. (*m*)	*I woke up.*
Il s'est douché.	*He had a shower.*
Elle s'est lavée.	*She washed / had a wash.*
Nous nous sommes promenés. (*mpl*)	*We went for a walk.*
Elles se sont recontrées.	*They met each other.*

B The past participle does not change its ending, however, where the reflexive pronoun is actually the *indirect* object of the verb. This happens:

• in phrases involving doing something for yourself or to yourself;

Elle s'est brossé les cheveux.   *She brushed her hair.*
(the direct object here is **les cheveux**)

- when the reflexive pronoun means *to/at each other.*
Ils se sont envoyé des   *They sent e-mails to each*
  courriers électroniques.   *other.*
Elles se sont téléphoné.   *They telephoned each other.*

C The question form with inversion is as follows:
S'est-elle assise?   *Has she sat down? / Did she*
                                    sit down?

D The negative (e.g. **ne … pas**) encloses both the reflexive
pronoun and the verb. In an inverted question it goes round
the reflexive pronoun, the verb and the subject pronoun.
Je ne me suis pas couché(e).   *I didn't go to bed.*
Elle ne s'est pas habillée.   *She didn't get dressed.*
Ne s'est-elle pas encore levée?   *Hasn't she got up yet?*

exercise

**Change the following present tense sentences into the perfect
tense. The basic past participles to use are in the box.**

E.g. Il se lève. → Il s'est levé.
a Tu te reposes.
b Ils s'arrêtent.
c Nous nous asseyons.
d Vous vous dépêchez.
e Elle s'ennuie.

assis	arrêté
dépêché	
reposé	ennuyé

There are important points to remember concerning past participle agreement when reflexive verbs are used in the perfect and other compound tenses.

A The past participle agrees with any preceding direct object in number and gender. This is called agreement of the past participle, and occurs with all compound tenses in a number of constructions.

B In the perfect tense the direct and indirect object pronouns are placed immediately before **avoir**. The past participle must agree with any *direct* object pronoun (but not with indirect object pronouns or the pronoun **en**).

Ce livre, tu l'as acheté?	*That book – did you buy it?*
Ces journaux, vous **les** avez lus?	*These papers – have you read them?*
Marie-Pierre était là, vous **lui** avez parlé?	*Marie-Pierre was here, did you speak to her?*
J'en ai acheté. (des disquettes, fpl)	*I've bought some. (floppy disks)*

The following table shows all forms of past participle agreement.

Masculine singular	Le livre? → Oui. Je l'ai acheté.	*I bought it.*
Feminine singular	La voiture? → Oui. Je l'ai achet**ée**.	*I bought it.*
Masculine plural	Les journaux? → Oui. Je les ai achet**és**.	*I bought them.*
Feminine plural	Les oranges? → Oui. Je les ai achet**ées**.	*I bought them.*

C This rule also applies in questions, including those that begin with **quel** (**quels/quelle/quelles**), **combien de** and (**lequel** (**lesquels/laquelle/lesquelles**).

Quelle voiture as-tu vu<u>e</u>?	*Which car did you see?*
Quels journaux as-tu acheté<u>s</u>?	*Which newspapers did you buy?*
Combien de livres a-t-elle acheté<u>s</u>?	*How many books did she buy?*
Laquelle as-tu acheté<u>e</u>?	*Which one did you buy?*
Lesquels avez-vous vu<u>s</u>?	*Which ones did you see?*

D Agreement also occurs when the relative pronoun **que** meaning *who(m)*, *that* or *which* comes before a verb in the perfect tense.

Les articles que tu as écrit<u>s</u> sont très intéressants.	*The articles (that) you wrote are very interesting.*
Les disquettes que j'ai acheté<u>es</u> sont sur mon bureau.	*The floppy disks I bought are on my desk.*

exercise

Complete the following sentences using the verb in brackets.

E.g. Où sont les documents que Maurice a (préparer)? →
Où sont les documents que Maurice a *préparés*?

a Combien de disquettes avez-vous (acheter)?
b Quel ordinateur a-t-il (utiliser)?
c Lesquels as-tu (laver)?
d Où est la lettre que j'ai (recevoir)?

The imperfect tense is used in description and to refer to repeated actions in the past.

A The imperfect tense is formed from the **nous** form of the present tense. You remove the **-ons** ending, then add the appropriate imperfect tense ending.

aller *to go* → nous allons → all-

The pronunciation is the same for -**ais**, -**ait** and -**aient**.

ALLER *to go*	
j'all**ais**	nous all**ions**
tu all**ais**	vous all**iez**
il/elle all**ait**	ils/elles all**aient**

The spelling change that affects **-er** verbs with stems ending in **-g** or **-c** in the present tense also applies in the imperfect in all persons except the **nous** and **vous** forms, e.g. **je mangeais** *I was eating*, **il lançait** *he threw*.

Être is irregular in the imperfect.

ÊTRE *to be*	
j'étais	nous étions
tu étais	vous étiez
il/elle était	ils/elles étaient

The imperfect tense has several meanings in French. It can be used:

• to describe regular or repeated actions in the past, in the sense of *used to*

Tous les samedis Claudine retrouvait son amie.	*Every Saturday Claudine met / used to meet / would meet her friend.*	**129** imperfect tense **64**

- to describe a continuous action in the past

Elles regardaient la télévision.	*They were watching television.*
Il lisait le journal.	*He was reading the paper.*

- to describe conditions, circumstances or a state of mind, possibly when something else occurred

Il pleuvait quand je suis arrivé.	*It was raining when I arrived.*

The following English pluperfects are translated by the imperfect in French, using **depuis** and **venir de**.

J'y travaillais depuis trois ans.	*I had worked there for three years.*
Je venais d'arriver.	*I had just arrived.*

exercise

Rewrite the following sentences in the imperfect tense.

E.g. Je mange une orange tous les jours. → Je mangeais une orange tous les jours.

a Ils prennent souvent le train.

b D'habitude, vous finissez votre travail avant de sortir.

c De temps en temps, je joue au tennis.

d Je me couche généralement vers minuit.

e Je travaille à l'hôpital.

f Elles rentrent à six heures à la maison.

The imperfect tense is used in description and to refer to repeated actions in the past.

A You will need to use both the perfect and imperfect tenses when referring to what happened in the past. The perfect is generally used to express single actions or events. The imperfect expresses (a) regular or repeated action, (b) a continuous action and (c) what was happening, conditions, circumstances or a state of mind (perhaps when something else occurred). These examples show their contrasting use.

• regular or repeated action (imperfect), one-off action or event (perfect)

Paul allait souvent en France. (repeated action) — *Paul often used to go to France.*

Moi, j'y suis allé une fois. (single action) — *I myself only went once.*

• continuous action (imperfect)

Jean regardait la télévision. — *Jean was watching television.*

Je travaillais à l'ordinateur. — *I was working on the computer.*

• what was happening (imperfect) when something else occurred (perfect)

Elisabeth faisait le ménage quand le téléphone a sonné. — *Elisabeth was doing the housework when the telephone rang.*

Claudine regardait un film à la télévision quand Bernard a frappé à la porte. *Claudine was watching a film on television when Bernard knocked at the door.*

Il neigeait quand nous sommes partis. *It was snowing when we left.*

J'ai mis un pullover parce que j'avais froid. *I put on a sweater because I was cold.*

Je suis allé voir le médecin parce que j'étais malade. *I went to see the doctor because I was ill.*

B If two events occurred at the same time, or two actions were taking place simultaneously, the same tense is used for both verbs.

Jean est arrivé et Pierre est parti. *Jean arrived and Pierre left.*

Michel nageait pendant que sa sœur se reposait sur la plage. *Michel was swimming while his sister relaxed on the beach.*

exercise

Complete the following sentences with the appropriate form of the perfect or imperfect tense of the verbs shown.

E.g. Il _____ quand son fils _____ . (dormir, appeler) →
Il *dormait* quand son fils *a appelé*.

a Je _____ quand le téléphone _____ . (lire, sonner)
b Elle _____ la radio quand quelqu'un _____ à la porte. (écouter, frapper)
c Pendant que nous _____ des courses (*shopping*), j'_____ mon porte-monnaie. (faire, perdre)

The pluperfect is a compound tense conjugated with *avoir* and *être* and is used to say what had happened.

The pluperfect tense is formed using the imperfect tense of **avoir** or être and a past participle.

A All verbs that take **avoir** in the perfect tense do so in the pluperfect tense.

TRAVAILLER *to work*	
j'avais travaillé	nous avions travaillé
tu avais travaillé	vous aviez travaillé
il/elle avait travaillé	ils/elles avaient travaillé

Elle avait travaillé toute   *She had worked all day.*
la journée.

The rules for the agreement of the past participle with any preceding direct object are the same as for the perfect tense.

B All verbs that take **être** in the perfect tense also do so in the pluperfect tense. The rules for past participle agree-

SORTIR *to go out*	
j'étais sorti(e)	nous étions sorti(e)s
tu étais sorti(e)	vous étiez sorti(e)(s)(es)
il/elle était sorti(e)	ils/elles étaient sorti(e)s

ment with the subject are also the same.

Elle était sortie avant lui.   *She had gone out before him.*

Reflexive verbs, as in the perfect tense, also take **être** in the pluperfect tense, and the reflexive pronoun changes according to the subject of the verb.

Je m'étais déjà couché quand tu as téléphoné.	*I had already gone to bed when you phoned.*

The pluperfect tense often occurs with other past tenses, and expresses an earlier event.

Quand nous sommes arrivés au restaurant, il avait déjà fini son repas.	*When we arrived at the restaurant, he had already finished his meal.*
Je pensais que tu avais acheté les livres.	*I thought you had bought the books.*
J'avais oublié qu'elle était végétarienne.	*I had forgotten that she was a vegetarian.*

exercise

Insert the correct form of *avoir* or *être* to form the pluperfect in the following sentences.

E.g. Elle _____ sortie quand vous la cherchiez. →
Elle *était* sortie quand vous la cherchiez.

a Il _____ fini son travail avant de partir.
b Elle _____ partie sans dire au revoir.
c Tu t'_____ couché tôt ce soir-là.
d Ils _____ déjà vu le film au cinéma avant de le louer en vidéo.
e J'_____ trop mangé à midi pour dîner le soir.
f Nous _____ allés voir des amis quand on a eu l'accident.

The past historic tense is used in written but rarely in spoken French to describe past actions and events.

A Formation

• All -er verbs follow the same pattern. Begin by removing the -er, then add the appropriate -a ending:

PARLER *to speak* (**-a** endings)	
je parl**ai**	nous parl**âmes**
tu parl**as**	vous parl**âtes**
il/elle parl**a**	ils/elles parl**èrent**

Il parla à l'agent de police.
He spoke to the policeman.

• All regular -ir verbs, all regular -re verbs, and some irregular verbs take the -i endings.

VENDRE *to sell* (**-i** endings)	
je vend**is**	nous vend**îmes**
tu vend**is**	vous vend**îtes**
il/elle vend**it**	ils/elles vend**irent**

Elle vendit sa voiture.
She sold her car.

Also **faire** (il fit), **dire** (il dit), **mettre** (il mit), **prendre** (il prit), **voir** (il vit), **rire** (il rit) and **s'asseoir** (il s'assit), etc.

• The -u endings are used for irregular -ir and -re verbs whose past participle ends in -u, and for **être** (**voir** and **battre** are exceptions: they follow the pattern illustrated by **vendre** above).

LIRE *to read* (**-u** endings)	
je l**us**	nous l**ûmes**
tu l**us**	vous l**ûtes**
il/elle l**ut**	ils/elles l**urent**

L'agent put arrêter le voleur.   *The officer was able to arrest the thief.*

Also **avoir (il eut)**, **boire (il but)**, **croire (il crut)**, **devoir (il dut)**, **pouvoir (il put)**, **savoir (il sut)** and **vouloir (il voulut)**, etc.

• **Venir, tenir** and their compounds have this pattern in the past historic.

Il vint me voir.
He came to see me.

VENIR *to come*	
je v**ins**	nous v**înmes**
tu v**ins**	vous v**întes**
il/elle v**int**	ils/elles v**inrent**

When a verb stem ends in -c or -g this changes to -ç or -g before an **a**, an **â** or a **u**: **je lançai** *I threw*, **il mangea** *he ate*, **ils reçurent** *they received*.

B The past historic is a narrative tense found in books, newspapers, magazines and official documents to describe completed events in the past. In speech and in less formal writing the perfect tense takes its place.

exercise

Change the verb from the past historic into the perfect tense.

E.g. **Ils furent frappés de panique.** → **Ils *ont été* frappés de panique.**

a Ils frappèrent à la porte.
b Elle attendit le train.
c Je choisis une chemise bleue.
d Il perdit sa clé.
e Il finit son travail.
f Ils répondirent à ma question.

The future tense is used to talk about what will or is going to happen.

A The future tense of most regular and many irregular verbs is formed by using the infinitive as the stem, and adding the future tense endings (-**re** verbs drop the final -**e** before adding the endings).

ARRIVER *to arrive*	
j'arriver**ai**	nous arriver**ons**
tu arriver**as**	vous arriver**ez**
il/elle arriver**a**	ils/elles arriver**ont**

Je vendrai ma voiture.   *I will / am going to sell my car.*

Most -**er** verbs that have a spelling change in the present tense maintain the change in the future tense. This occurs in all persons.

j'ach**è**terai   *I will sell*   j'appe**ll**erai   *I will call*

B Some verbs are irregular in the future tense and do not form their stem from the infinitive, for example:

Infinitive	Future	Infinitive	Future
aller *to go*	j'irai	mettre *to put*	je mettrai
avoir *to have*	j'aurai	pouvoir *to be able*	je pourrai
devoir *to have to*	je devrai	savoir *to know*	je saurai
envoyer *to send*	j'enverrai	venir *to come*	je viendrai
être *to be*	je serai	voir *to see*	je verrai
faire *to make, to do*	je ferai	vouloir *to want*	je voudrai

C Ways of expressing the future in French

• with the future tense:

L'année prochaine je changerai d'emploi.	*Next year I'll change jobs.*

With **quand** the future tense is used in French (present tense in English).

Quand vous arriverez appelez-moi.	*When you arrive call me.*

• with the simple future tense (**aller** + infinitive), mainly for the immediate future:

Je vais te le montrer.	*I'll show you it.*

• with the present tense:

Le spectacle commence à sept heures.	*The show starts at seven o'clock.*
Je pars demain.	*I'm leaving tomorrow.*

exercise

Say what Andrew will do on holiday, using the future tense of the verb in brackets.

E.g. (aller) en France → *Il ira* en France.

a (faire) du camping

b (louer) un vélo

c (écrire) des cartes postales

d (acheter) des souvenirs

e (visiter) des endroits intéressants

f (téléphoner) à sa mère

The future perfect is a compound tense conjugated with *avoir* or *être*. It is used to say what will have happened.

A The future perfect tense is formed with the future tense of **avoir** or **être** and a past participle.

• All verbs that take **avoir** in the perfect tense do so in the future perfect.

ACHETER *to buy*	
j'aurai acheté	nous aurons acheté
tu auras acheté	vous aurez acheté
il/elle aura acheté	ils/elles auront acheté

Il aura acheté le cadeau avant mardi.　　*He will have bought the present by Tuesday.*

The rules for the agreement of the past participle with any preceding direct object are the same as for the perfect tense.

• All verbs that take **être** in the perfect tense also do so in the future perfect. The rules for past participle agreement

PARTIR *to leave*	
je serai parti(e)	nous serons parti(e)s
tu seras parti(e)	vous serez parti(e)(s)(es)
il/elle sera parti(e)	ils/elles seront parti(e)s

with the subject are also the same.

Tu seras parti avant juillet.　　*You will have left by July.*

• Reflexive verbs again take **être,** and rules for past participle agreement with the subject also apply as in the perfect.
Je me serai levé(e) tôt.　　*I will have got up early.*

B You use the future perfect to talk about a future action which will be completed before another future action.

Ils auront fini quand vous arriverez.

They will have finished when / by the time you arrive.

• It is used after certain time expressions, such as **quand** *when*, **après que** *after*, **aussitôt que** *as soon as*, **dès que** *as soon as* and **tant que** *as long as*.

Aussitôt qu'il aura fini, nous sortirons.

As soon as he has finished, we will go out.

There is a difference in tenses used in English and French. In English we use the perfect tense, whereas in French the future perfect is used.

exercise

Match the following sentence halves to make whole sentences.

E.g. **Ils seront + arrivés maintenant. → Ils seront arrivés maintenant.**

a Il sera	1 fini mon travail.
b J'aurai	2 rentrées de Paris.
c Elles seront	3 parti de bonne heure.
d Vous aurez	4 resté chez toi.
e Tu seras	5 acheté des fleurs.

The conditional is used mainly to describe what would happen:
If I were rich I would buy a house.

A The conditional is formed from the future stem (regular or irregular) of a verb and the imperfect tense endings.

Si j'avais assez d'argent, j'achèterais une nouvelle voiture.	*If I had enough money, I would buy a new car.*

TROUVER *to find*	
je trouver**ais**	nous trouver**ions**
tu trouver**ais**	vous trouver**iez**
il/elle trouver**ait**	ils/elles trouver**aient**

Most -**er** verbs that have a spelling change in the present tense maintain the change in the conditional, in all persons, as they do in the future tense.

j'ach**è**terais   *I would sell*   j'appe**ll**erais   *I would call*

B Use of the conditional

- The main purpose of the conditional is to say what *would happen.*

J'achèterais ce livre si j'avais assez d'argent.	*I would buy this book if I had enough money.*
Si j'étais malade, j'irais chez le médecin.	*If I was ill, I would go to the doctor's.*

- It is used to make politc statements.

Je vous serais très reconnaissant *I would be very grateful if*
si vous pouviez venir. *you could come.*

Je préférerais y aller demain. *I would prefer to go*
tomorrow.

- The conditional of **vouloir** and **pouvoir** is used to make polite requests.

Je voudrais un café, s'il vous *I would like a coffee,*
plaît. *please.*

Pourriez-vous m'aider, s'il vous *Could you help me, please?*
plaît?

- The conditional of **pouvoir** is used to express possibility.

Elle pourrait arriver lundi. *She could (might) arrive on*
Monday.

- The conditional of **devoir** is used to say that someone should or ought to do something.

Tu devrais te reposer. *You ought to (should) rest.*

exercise

Write out the conditional forms of the verbs indicated.

a avoir	il _____		**f** finir	elle _____
b devoir	je _____		**g** être	je _____
c prendre	nous _____		**h** faire	elles _____
d pouvoir	vous _____		**i** acheter	vous _____
e vouloir	tu _____		**j** venir	il _____

The conditional perfect is a compound tense conjugated with *avoir* or *être*, and is used to say would what have happened.

A The conditional perfect is formed with the conditional of **avoir** or **être** and a past participle.

• All verbs that take **avoir** in the perfect do so in the conditional perfect.

FINIR *to finish*	
j'aurais fini	nous aurions fini
tu aurais fini	vous auriez fini
il/elle aurait fini	ils/elles auraient fini

Il aurait fini, s'il avait eu le temps.   *He would have finished,*
if he had had the time.

The rules for the agreement of the past participle with any preceding direct object are as for the perfect tense.

• All verbs that take **être** in the perfect tense also do so in the conditional perfect. The rules for past participle

ARRIVER *to arrive*	
je serais arrivé(e)	nous serions arrivé(e)s
tu serais arrivé(e)	vous seriez arrivé(e)(s)(es)
il/elle serait arrivé(e)	ils/elles seraient arrivé(e)s

agreement with the subject are also the same.

Elle serait arrivée, mais son train   *She would have arrived,*
était en retard.   *but her train was late.*

- Reflexive verbs again take **être**, and rules for the past
  participle agreement with the subject also apply as in the
  perfect.

Elle se serait douchée, mais elle
  était trop pressée.

*She would have showered
  but she was in too
  much of a hurry.*

B The conditional perfect is used to describe what would have
happened if something else or circumstances had not
prevented it.

Elle serait partie, mais il neigeait.   *She would have left but it
  was snowing.*

- You use the conditional perfect of modal verbs to describe
  what you *should have*, *could have* or *would have liked to
  do*.

J'aurais dû lire l'article.   *I should have read the
  article.*

J'aurais pu lire l'article.   *I could have read the
  article.*

J'aurais voulu lire l'article.   *I would have liked to
  read the article.*

exercise

See exercise 53 in 'More practice'.

There are certain rules about which tenses to use in sentences with *si* meaning *if, provided that* or *whether*.

A When you use **si**, the rules concerning tenses are as follows.

- main clause + future tense; **si** clause + present tense

Je pourrai porter cette robe ce soir, si je l'achète. | *I will be able to wear this dress this evening, if I buy it.*

- main clause + conditional; **si** clause + imperfect tense

J'achèterais une robe en soie, si j'avais assez d'argent. | *I would buy a silk dress, if I had enough money.*

- main clause + conditional perfect; **si** clause + pluperfect tense

J'aurais pu porter la robe ce soir, si je l'avais achetée. | *I would have been able to wear the dress this evening, if I had bought it.*

In most cases the **si** clause can also come before the main clause.

Si elle n'est pas trop chère, j'achèterai cette robe. | *If it is not too expensive I will buy this dress.*

B Si can mean *if* in the sense of *provided that*:

J'achèterai cette robe si elle n'est pas trop chère. | *I will buy this dress if it is not too expensive.*

C Si + imperfect tense can mean *Suppose...?, How about...?* or *What if...?*

Si nous partions maintenant? | *Suppose / What if we left now?*

D *If (only)* can be translated by **si (seulement)** + the imperfect or pluperfect tense.

Si seulement tu pouvais rester!	*If only you could / were able to stay!*
Si (seulement) j'avais su!	*If (only) I had known!*

E **Si** meaning *whether* to introduce an indirect question (i.e. used as a subordinating conjunction) can be followed by any tense.

Je me demande si elle vient.	*I wonder if/whether she's coming.*
Je me demande s'il est arrivé.	*I wonder if/whether he's arrived.*

Si shortens to **s'** only when followed by **il** and **ils**. **Si on** can become **si l'on**.

On n'entre pas si l'on ne porte pas de veston.	*They don't let you in if you're not wearing a jacket.*

exercise

Put each verb in brackets into the correct tense.

a Si j' (travailler), j' (faire) des progrès.

If I had worked, I would have made progress.

b Si j' (avoir) beaucoup d'argent j' (acheter) une maison en France.

If I had a lot of money I would buy a house in France.

c Si je (finir) mon travail, je (pouvoir) sortir plus tard.

If I finish my work, I will be able to go out later.

The perfect infinitive is used to say *after having done...*, and following certain verbs.

A When a sentence describes two consecutive actions carried out by the same person, you can use **après avoir/être** + past participle. For **avoir** verbs the rules for agreement of the past participle with any preceding direct object are the same as for the perfect tense. All verbs that take **être** in the perfect tense again do so here, and the rules for past participle agreement with the subject are also the same.

• With **avoir** verbs, use **après** + **avoir** + past participle.

Après avoir fini son travail, elle est rentrée chez elle.	*After finishing her work, she went home.*

• With **être** verbs, use **après** + **être** + past participle.

Après être arrivée à la gare, elle a acheté un billet.	*After arriving at the station, she bought a ticket.*
Après être tombé, il a commencé à pleurer.	*After falling, he began to cry.*

• With reflexive verbs the reflexive pronoun appears before **être**, and it must agree in number and gender with the subject of the clauses.

Après m'être réveillé(e), j'ai pris une tasse de thé.	*After waking up, I had a cup of tea.*
Après s'être levée, elle est partie.	*After getting up, she left.*

B The perfect infinitive is also used after certain verbs, mostly expressing attitude or memory, where again the subject of both clauses is the same.

Elle se souvenait d'avoir bien mangé chez Gaston.

She remembered eating well at Gaston's.

Other such verbs include: **être content de** *to be happy that*, **remercier de** *to thank for/that*, **regretter de** *to regret that*.

C The present participles of **avoir** (**ayant**) and **être** (**étant**) can also be used in this way with the past participle.

Ayant fini son travail, elle a quitté le bureau.

Having finished her work, she left the office.

Étant venue par le train, elle est arrivée la première.

Having come by train she arrived first.

exercise

Insert a suitable *après* construction from the box into the sentences below.

Après m'être reposé(e)   Après être arrivés   Après être arrivé
Après avoir appris

a _____ à conduire elle a acheté une voiture. *After learning to drive she bought a car.*

b _____ Jean nous a parlé de ses vacances. *After arriving Jean talked to us about his holidays.*

c _____ un peu j'ai continué à travailler. *After resting a little I continued to work.*

d _____ trop tard, nous avons raté le train. *After arriving too late, we missed the train.*

A passive construction is used when the subject of the verb is the person or thing not doing but receiving the action: *The present was given*.

A The French passive, like the English, is formed with an appropriate tense of the verb **être** *to be*, plus a past participle (which in French must agree with the subject). An active sentence containing a subject, verb and direct object can be changed into a passive sentence.

ACTIVE: Henri a envoyé la lettre. *Henri sent the letter.*
PASSIVE: La lettre a été envoyée par Henri. *The letter was sent by Henri.*

B This table shows the formation and meaning of the passive in several tenses.

Present	La pièce est repeinte chaque année.	*The room is repainted every year.*
Perfect	La pièce a été repeinte.	*The room has been repainted.*
Imperfect	La pièce était repeinte chaque année.	*The room was repainted every year.*
Pluperfect	La pièce avait été repeinte.	*The room had been repainted.*
Future	La pièce sera repeinte.	*The room will be repainted.*
Conditional	La pièce serait repeinte.	*The room would be repainted.*

In the present and imperfect tenses the past participle can sometimes be purely descriptive and give no indication of a particular action.

La voiture est vendue. *The car's sold.*

La pièce était peinte en bleu. *The room was painted blue.*

C In French the indirect object of a verb cannot become the subject of a passive clause, as it can in English, so another structure has to be used.

On lui a donné des nouvelles. *He was given some* (donner à) *news.*

On m'a parlé du projet. (parler à) *I was told about the project.*

D French often avoids the passive, and this can be done in several ways:

• by using **on** + an active verb (as in **C** above), or another active construction

On a écrit l'article. *The article has been written.*

Deux infirmières l'ont accompagné. *He was accompanied by two nurses.*

• by using a reflexive construction, adding a reflexive pronoun to the verb; this is most common in the **il(s)** and **elle(s)** forms

Les journaux se vendent ici. *Newspapers are sold here.*

Ce mot ne s'emploie pas. *This word is not used.*

exercise

See exercise 54 in 'More practice'.

In general terms, the subjunctive is used to express mood, attitude or uncertainty. It is usually introduced by *que*.

A The present subjunctive is formed by taking the **ils/elles** form of the present tense, removing the **-ent** and adding the appropriate subjunctive ending.

TROUVER *to find* present: ils **trouv**ent	FINIR *to finish* present: ils **finiss**ent	ATTENDRE *to wait* present: ils **attend**ent
que je trouv**e**	que je finiss**e**	que j'attend**e**
que tu trouv**es**	que tu finiss**es**	que tu attend**es**
qu'il/elle trouv**e**	qu'il/elle finiss**e**	qu'il/elle attend**e**
que nous trouv**ions**	que nous finiss**ions**	que nous attend**ions**
que vous trouv**iez**	que vous finiss**iez**	que vous attend**iez**
qu'ils/elles trouv**ent**	qu'ils/elles finiss**ent**	qu'ils/elles attend**ent**

B Avoir and être are irregular.

AVOIR *to have*		ÊTRE *to be*	
que j'aie	que nous ayons	que je sois	que nous soyions
que tu aies	que vous ayez	que tu sois	que vous soyez
qu'il/elle ait	qu'ils/elles aient	qu'il/elle soit	qu'ils/elles soient

C The present subjunctive stem of these verbs is irregular.

aller	qu'il <u>aille</u> (BUT nous <u>allions</u>, vous <u>alliez</u>)
faire	qu'il <u>fasse</u>
pouvoir	qu'il <u>puisse</u> (BUT nous <u>pouvions</u>, vous <u>pouviez</u>)
savoir	qu'il <u>sache</u>
vouloir	qu'il <u>veuille</u> (BUT nous <u>voulions</u>, vous <u>vouliez</u>)

D Some verbs are irregular only in the **nous** and **vous** forms, where they are identical to the imperfect (**qu'il boive** but **nous buvions, vous buviez**). Others include **croire** to *believe* (croie/croyions), **devoir** to *have to* (doive/devions), **mourir** to *die* (meure/mourions), **prendre** to *take* (prenne/prenions), **voir** to *see* (voie/voyions).

Verbs with spelling changes in the present indicative stem change also in the subjunctive, except those with stems ending in **-g** and **-c** (**manger** to *eat*, **commencer** to *start*) where the change for pronunciation is unnecessary.

exercise

Give the *je* and *vous* forms of the present subjunctive of the following verbs.

| **a** vouloir | **c** savoir | **e** boire |
| **b** aller | **d** venir | **f** être |

The perfect subjunctive is the subjunctive version of the perfect indicative.

A The perfect subjunctive is formed with the present subjunctive of **avoir** or être and a past participle.

TROUVER to *find*	ARRIVER *to arrive*
que j'**aie trouvé**	que je **sois arrivé(e)**
que tu **aies trouvé**	que tu **sois arrivé(e)**
qu'il/elle **ait trouvé**	qu'il/elle **soit arrivé(e)**
que nous **ayons trouvé**	que nous **soyons arrivé(e)s**
que vous **ayez trouvé**	que vous **soyez arrivé(e)(s)(es)**
qu'ils/elles **aient trouvé**	qu'ils/elles **soient arrivé(e)s**

The rules for agreement of the past participle with any preceding direct object are as for the perfect tense. All verbs that take **être** in the perfect tense do so in the perfect subjunctive, and the rules for past participle agreement with the subject are the same as in the perfect tense.

B Reflexive verbs again take **être,** and rules for past participle agreement with the subject apply as in the perfect tense.

SE LEVER *to get up, to stand up*	
que je me **sois levé(e)**	que nous nous **soyons levé(e)s**
que tu te **sois levé(e)**	que vous vous **soyez levé(e)(s)(es)**
qu'il/elle se **soit levé(e)**	qu'ils/elles se **soient levé(e)s**

'Quoique je sois contente qu'elle ait enfin trouvé un passe-temps
qui lui plaît, je regrette qu'il soit un peu dangereux'

exercise

Rewrite the following sentences in the perfect subjunctive, beginning each one with *Je suis content que...*

E.g. Nous (aller) au concert. *I'm pleased that we went to the concert.* Je suis contente que nous *soyions allés* au concert.

a Il (gagner) le prix. *I'm pleased that he has won the prize.*

b Elle (apprendre) à conduire. *I'm pleased that she has learned to drive.*

c Tu (se reposer) un peu. *I'm pleased that you've had a bit of a rest.*

d Vous (passer) le weekend chez eux. *I'm pleased that you have spent the weekend at their place.*

e Elles (aller) en vacances. *I'm pleased that they have gone on holiday.*

f Il (partir) à l'heure. *I'm pleased that he left on time.*

g Vous (parler) au curé. *I'm pleased that you have spoken to the priest.*

The subjunctive is used following verbs that express an emotion or an uncertainty. It is usually introduced by *que*.

A The subjunctive is used with verbs expressing wish, will, preference or desire (e.g. **aimer que** *to like that*, **désirer que** *to desire that*, **préférer que** *to prefer that*, **souhaiter que** *to wish that*, **vouloir que** *to want that*). **Espérer** *to hope* however is followed by the indicative.

Il veut que Guy **aille** au match.	*He wants Guy to go to the match.*
J'espère que tu pourras venir.	*I hope you will be able to come.*

B It is used after verbal phrases expressing pleasure, regret, concern or emotion.

Je suis content que vous puissiez venir.	*I'm pleased you can come.*
Je regrette qu'il soit si fâché.	*I'm sorry he's so angry.*

être heureux que *to be happy that*
être triste que *to be sad that*
être fier que *to be proud that*
être désolé que *to be sorry that*
être furieux que *to be furious that*
être fâché que *to be annoyed that*
être déçu que *to be disappointed that*
être surpris/étonné que *to be surprised/astonished that*
avoir peur que ... ne *to be afraid that*
avoir crainte que ... ne *to fear that*
craindre que ... ne *to fear that*

Where s   bove, **ne** is inserted before the verb that
follows.

C It is u   r verbs of doubt, uncertainty or denial, mainly
when be   d negatively or interrogatively.

Je do vienne.	*I doubt he is coming.*
Tu cro i vienne?	*Do you think he'll come?*
Je ne pe. pas qu'il vienne.	*I don't think he's coming.*

douter que *to doubt that*   nier que *to deny that*
(ne ... pas) croire que *(not) to believe that*
(ne ... pas) penser que *(not) to think that*
(ne ... pas) être sûr que *(not) to be sure that*

D It's also needed after verbs involving commands or
permission, and after **attendre que** *to wait until*.

Il permet que le match ait lieu.	*He's allowing the match to take place.*
Elle attend que le match soit fini.	*She's waiting until the match is over.*

When both clauses have the same subject, it is usual to use **de**
+ infinitive rather than **que** + subjunctive.

Elle est heureuse de savoir le résultat.	*She's pleased to know the result.*

exercise

See exercise 56 in 'More practice'.

The subjunctive is also used after certain subordinating conjunctions and impersonal expressions. It is introduced by *que*.

A The following conjunctions are followed by a verb in the subjunctive.

avant que ... je (**ne**) parte	*before I leave*
bien que je sache la vérité	*although I know the truth*
quoique je sache la vérité	*although I know the truth*
pour que je puisse rester chez moi	*so that / in order that I can stay at home*
afin que je puisse rester chez moi	*so that / in order that I can stay at home*
sans que je sois inquiet	*without my being worried*
à condition que tu y ailles avec moi	*provided that you go with me*
jusqu'à ce qu'elle arrive	*until she arrives*
de peur/crainte que tu **ne** viennes	*for fear that (in case) you don't come*
à moins que tu (**ne**) sois seul	*unless you are alone*

Avant que and **à moins que** can take a **ne** before the verb, and **de peur que** and **de crainte que** usually do so.

B De sorte/façon/manière que (*so that*) take the subjunctive when describing an intention, but the indicative when expressing a result.

C The subjunctive is also used with impersonal constructions that express opinion, necessity, possibility, doubt and denial.

Il **vaut mieux que** tu viennes.	*It's better that you come.*
Il **faut que** je le voies.	*I must / It is necessary that I see him.*
Il **se peut qu'il** revienne.	*It is possible that he will come back.*

il est (im)possible que	*it's (im)possible that*
il est peu probable que	*it's unlikely that*
c'est dommage que	*it's a pity that*
il n'est pas évident que	*it's not evident that*
il n'est pas certain/sûr que	*it's not certain/sure that*
il n'est pas vrai que	*it's not true that*
il semble que	*it seems that*

When some of these expressions are used positively they are followed by the indicative.

Il est vrai que vous avez raison. *It's true that you are right.*

Although **il semble que** is followed by the subjunctive, **il *me* semble que** *it seems to me that* is followed by the indicative.

exercise

Introduce each of the following sentences using the expression in brackets. They all require the subjunctive.

a Il fait ses devoirs. (Il est important que)

b Vous travaillez. (Il faut que)

c Il réussit. (Il est impossible que)

The subjunctive is used in relative clauses after a superlative expression, a negative or an indefinite pronoun, and also certain imperatives.

A The subjunctive is used after a negative or indefinite pronoun + **qui** or **que**. However, if the pronoun is used in a positive sense, the indicative is used.

Je ne sais rien qui puisse vous aider.	*I don't know of anything that could help you.*
Il n'y a rien que je puisse vous dire.	*There is nothing I can tell you.*
Il n'y a personne qui puisse vous aider.	*There's no one who can help you.*
Il y a quelqu'un qui puisse le faire?	*Is there anyone who can do it?*
Je cherche quelqu'un qui sache parler français.	*I am looking for someone who can speak French. (i.e. I haven't found him/her yet.)*

BUT

Je connais quelqu'un qui sait parler français.	*I know someone who can speak French.*
Il y a quelqu'un qui peut le faire.	*There is someone who can do it.*

B The subjunctive occurs after a superlative, and after **dernier** *last*, **premier** *first* and **seul** *only*.

use of the subjunctive (3)

79

C'est la voiture la plus puissante que j'aie jamais conduite.	*It's the most powerful car I've ever driven.*
C'est le meilleur livre qu'il ait jamais lu.	*It's the best book he has ever read.*
Elle est la seule qui puisse le faire.	*She is the only one who can do it.*

C The subjunctive is used after certain indefinite expressions.

Qui que vous soyez, vous n'avez pas le droit d'entrer.	*Whoever you are, you don't have the right to enter.*

Other examples of such expressions are:

quoi que tu fasses	*whatever you do*
où que tu ailles	*wherever you go*
d'où que vous veniez	*wherever you come from*
à qui que vous parliez	*whoever you talk to*
quelle que soit ton opinion*	*whatever your opinion (may be)* (i.e. *whatever* in the sense of *which ever*)

*__Quel que__ is used with a noun and must agree with it in number and gender.

exercise

See exercise 57 in 'More practice'.

Conjunctions link items to form longer sentences. They fall into three categories: coordinating, subordinating and correlating conjunctions.

Coordinating conjunctions link sentences, clauses, phrases or words of equal status, e.g. main clause + main clause, subordinate clause + subordinate clause, noun + noun, comparative phrases, etc.

J'ai fini mon travail **puis** j'ai quitté le bureau.	*I finished my work then I left the office.*

A The main coordinating conjunctions are:

ainsi *thus, so, therefore*	ensuite *then*
alors *then, so*	et *and*
au contraire *on the contrary*	mais *but*
aussi *so, therefore*	néanmoins *nevertheless*
car *because*	or *however*
c'est-à-dire *that is to say*	que *than*
c'est pourquoi *that's why*	ou *or*
d'ailleurs *besides*	pourtant *however*
donc *so*	puis *then*
en effet *indeed*	toutefois *however*

B Main clause + main clause

Le train est arrivé **et** je suis monté dedans.	*The train arrived and I got on.*

Donc can be placed either between two main clauses or within the second one.

Il n'était pas content, donc je suis allé le voir / je suis donc allé le voir.	*He wasn't happy, so I went to see him.*

C Subordinate clause + subordinate clause

Cette femme, qui était renommée **mais** qui était mécontente, s'est retirée du monde.	*This woman, who was famous but who was unhappy, withdrew from the world.*

D Noun + noun

Elle est devenue vedette du cinéma **puis** femme politique.	*She became a film star then a politician.*

E Comparative

Elle était plus tolérante **que** lui.	*She was more tolerant than him.*

exercise

Complete each sentence using one of the three conjunctions in the box next to each set. Then translate each sentence into English.

a Moi, je l'aime, mais elle _____ ne l'aime pas du tout.

b Il neigeait _____ je n'y suis pas allé.

c Il voulait venir _____ il n'avait pas le temps.

> donc
> mais
> au contraire

d Il a fait la cuisine _____ moi j'ai fait la vaisselle.

e Il l'a réparée, _____ nous avons pu partir.

f Je ne veux pas l'acheter, _____ je n'ai pas assez d'argent.

> d'ailleurs
> puis
> ainsi

Conjunctions link items to form longer sentences. They fall into three categories: coordinating, subordinating and correlating conjunctions.

A Subordinating conjunctions link main and subordinate clauses. The subordinate clause adds more information to the content or message of the main clause.

J'ai dit **que** je n'avais pas le temps.	*I said that I didn't have the time.*
Elle l'a félicité **parce qu**'il avait fini.	*She congratulated him because he had finished.*
J'ai rangé sa chambre **pendant qu**'elle jouait en bas.	*I tidied her room while she played downstairs.*
Vous voulez manger **avant qu**'on (**ne**) sorte?	*Do you want to eat before we go out?*

The main subordinating conjunctions are:

à moins que … (ne) *unless*   jusqu'à ce que *until*
afin que *so that*   lorsque *when*
après que *after*   parce que *because*
aussitôt que *as soon as*   pendant que *while*
avant que … (ne) *before*   pour que *so that*
bien que *although*   puisque *since (= because)*
comme *as (= because)*   quand *when*
de crainte que … ne *for fear that*   quoique *although*
de façon / de sorte que *so that*   que *that*
de peur que … ne *for fear that*   si *if, whether*
depuis que *since*   tandis que *while*
dès que *as soon as*

B Correlating conjunctions link several items together (e.g. to make a double subject or object).

Et les patrons et les employés
étaient contre la nouvelle loi.

*Both employers and
employees were
against the new law.*

Vous pouvez **ou** venir **ou** rester.

*You can either come or
stay.*

The main correlating conjunctions are:

et ... et   *both ... and*   ou ... ou *either ... or*
ne ... ni ... ni   *neither ... nor*

exercise

**Complete the following story with the conjunctions indicated.
Look back at Unit 80 if necessary.**

(*As*) il faisait mauvais en juillet, nous avons décidé de passer
un weekend en France. (*While*) je faisais ma valise, mon mari
m'a dit (*that*) il ne trouvait pas son passeport. À mon avis le
passeport était (*either*) dans le bureau (*or*) dans le tiroir. (*So*)
je lui ai demandé (*whether*) il avait cherché dans le bureau.
Pas encore. «Dis-le-moi (*as soon as*) tu le trouveras.»

There is a range of negatives in French which express *not*, *nothing*, *never*, *no more*, no longer, etc.

A Most negatives in French consist of two words placed on either side of the conjugated verb, enclosing also any reflexive and object pronouns (and any subject pronouns in questions). The most common is **ne … pas**. **Ne** becomes **n'** when the next word begins with a vowel.

Je n'y vais pas souvent.	*I don't go there often.*

B The most common negatives are:

Group A	Group B
ne … guère *hardly*	ne … aucun(e)* *not any, none*
ne … jamais *never*	ne … ni … ni *neither … nor*
ne … pas *not*	ne … personne *nobody*
ne … plus *no longer*	ne … que *only*
ne … rien *nothing*	

*Aucun(e) agrees in number and gender with the noun it relates to.

Elle ne va jamais au théâtre.	*She never goes to the theatre.*
Vous n'avez rien dans votre sac.	*You have nothing in your bag.*
Je ne vais plus à la messe.	*I don't go to church any more.*
N'a-t-il que deux enfants?	*Has he only got two children?*

| Elles n'aiment personne. | *They don't like anybody.* |
| Il n'a aucune idée. | *He hasn't got any idea.* |

C Aucun(e), **jamais**, **personne**, **rien**, and **ni … ni** can stand at the beginning of a clause, with **ne** then following in its usual place.

Personne ne répond.	*Nobody's answering.*
Rien n'est impossible.	*Nothing is impossible.*
Ni Jean ni Hélène ne sont venus.	*Neither Jean nor Hélène has come.*

D Aucun(e), **jamais**, **rien** and **personne** can be used alone without a verb.

| Vous buvez de la bière? Jamais. | *Do you drink beer? Never.* |
| Qui vient à la plage? Personne. | *Who's coming to the beach? Nobody.* |

E When an infinitive is being negated it is preceded by the negative, except for those negatives in Group B above, which enclose it.

| Je te conseille de ne pas nager ici. | *I advise you not to swim here.* |
| Je te promets de ne voir personne. | *I promise you not to see anyone.* |

exercise

See exercise 58 in 'More practice'.

There are rules governing word order when using negatives with compound tenses. French negatives can be combined.

A Verbs in compound tenses are made negative by adding **ne** before the auxiliary verb (**avoir** or **être**) and **pas** (etc.) after it: **ne** + auxiliary + **pas** + past participle. If there is an object pronoun it is enclosed within the negative.

J'ai travaillé. → Je n'ai pas travaillé.	*I have worked.* → *I have not worked.*
Il est arrivé. → Il n'est pas arrivé.	*He has arrived.* → *He has not arrived.*
Je ne l'ai pas vue.	*I didn't see her.*

B When negating reflexive verbs both the reflexive pronoun and the auxiliary verb are enclosed by the negative.

Je ne me suis pas dépêché.	*I did not hurry.*
Elle ne s'est pas couchée.	*She has not gone to bed.*

C In negative questions where the subject and auxiliary verb are inverted, the negative encloses the auxiliary verb and the subject pronoun, and also any object pronoun. With reflexive verbs the reflexive pronoun is enclosed as well.

N'a-t-il rien dit?	*Didn't he say anything?*
Ne les a-t-elle pas pris?	*Didn't she take them?*
Ne s'est-elle pas annoncée?	*Didn't she say she was there?*

D The negatives in Group B in Unit 82 have a different order in both statements and questions. The order is **ne** + auxiliary + past participle + **pas** (etc.).

Je n'ai vu personne.   *I haven't seen anyone.*
N'as-tu acheté que trois kilos?   *Did you only buy three kilos?*

E Negatives can combine in various ways: **ne … plus rien** *no longer anything*, **ne … jamais personne** *never anyone*, **ne … jamais rien** *never anything*, **ne … plus que** *nothing else but*, **ne … plus jamais** *never any more*, **ne … plus personne** *never anyone any more*, **ne … jamais que** *only ever*.

Elle ne fait jamais rien.   *She never does anything.*
Il ne voit plus personne.   *He never sees anyone any more.*

Il ne me donne plus jamais   *He never gives me*
  de fleurs.   *flowers any more.*

exercise

Answer the following questions in the negative. The answer is given in English to help you.

E.g. Vous avez fini? *Have you finished?* Non, je n'ai pas fini.

a A-t-il vu Pierre? *No, he has not seen him.*
b Tu es parti avant minuit? *No, I did not leave before midnight.*
c Est-ce qu'il sera arrivé à l'heure? *No, he will not have arrived on time.*
d Elle s'est maquillée avant de sortir? *No, she did not put on her make-up before going out.*

84 asking questions (1)

There are three ways of forming a simple question in French.

A A statement can be made into a question by raising your intonation at the end of the sentence.

Vous aimez le fromage. *You like cheese.*
→ Vous aimez le fromage? *Do you like cheese?*

B A statement can also be changed into a question by placing **Est-ce que …** at the beginning.

Tu as une voiture. *You have a car.*
→ Est-ce que tu as une voiture? *Do you have a car?*
Vous avez mangé. *You have eaten.*
→ Est-ce que vous avez mangé? *Have you eaten?*
Ils vont partir. *They're going to leave.*
→ Est-ce qu'ils vont partir? *Are they going to leave?*

C More formal questions can be formed by reversing (inverting) the subject pronoun and the conjugated verb (in compound tenses the auxiliary verb **avoir** or **être**). This method is not common in informal speech.

Elle fait des études de langues. *She's studying languages.*
→ Fait-elle des études de langues? *Is she studying languages?*

Vous voulez manger. *You want to eat.*
→ Voulez-vous manger? *Do you want to eat?*
Vous avez fini. *You have finished.*
→ Avez-vous fini? *Have you finished?*
Il était déjà rentré quand je suis arrivé. *He had already gone home when I arrived.*

$\rightarrow$ Était-il déjà rentré quand je   *Had he already gone*
suis arrivé?   *home when I arrived?*

When forming a question like this with the third-person singular (**il** or **elle**), and the conjugated verb ends in a vowel, an extra **t** is added to ease pronunciation. This is often necessary in compound tenses.

Joue-t-elle au tennis?   *Does she play tennis?*
Va-t-il finir son travail?   *Is he going to finish his work?*
A-t-elle écrit la lettre?   *Has she written the letter?*
Sera-t-il déjà parti quand   *Will he have already left*
j'arriverai?   *when I arrive?*

exercise

Find three ways of changing each of the following statements into a question.

E.g. Vous avez mangé à midi.

$\rightarrow$ Vous avez mangé à midi?
$\rightarrow$ Est-ce que vous avez mangé à midi?
$\rightarrow$ Avez-vous mangé à midi?

a Tu achètes un ordinateur.
b Il est pharmacien.
c Elle adore le théâtre.
d Vous aimez le vin.
e Ils vont en ville.

There are a number of words you can use to find out what you need to know, for example *Why...?*, *Where...?*, *When...?*, *How...?*

A There are a number of key words (interrogatives) you can use to find out specific information: **quand?** *when?*, **pourquoi?** *why?*, **où?** *where?*, **comment?** *how?* and **combien (de)?** *how much / how many?*

Ils arrivent quand?	*When do they arrive?*
Pourquoi est-ce que tu pleures?	*Why are you crying?*
Où est la poste?	*Where is the post office?*
Comment voyagez-vous?	*How are you travelling?*
Ça coûte combien?	*How much does it cost?*
Vous gagnez combien (d'argent)?	*How much (money) do you earn?*

B As these examples show, there are three ways of forming questions when using these words, which are broadly in line with the simple question forms seen in Unit 84. You can:

• add the interrogative after the statement (**Ils arrivent *quand*? Tu veux manger *où*?**). (**Pourquoi** however cannot be used this way.)

• add the interrogative at the beginning of a question that uses **est-ce que** (***Pourquoi* est-ce que tu pleures? *Quand* est-ce que tu veux manger?**)

• place the interrogative at the beginning of the question and invert the subject and verb (***Où* est la poste? *Où* est-il? *Quand* va-t-elle arriver?**).

C If you want to ask *Which...?* or *What...?* plus a noun, you use the appropriate form of the interrogative adjective **quel?** This agrees in gender and number with the noun that follows it.

	Singular	Plural
Masculine	quel	quels
Feminine	quelle	quelles

Quel livre lisez-vous?	*Which book are you reading?*
Quelle date préférerait-il?	*Which date would he prefer?*

D Some of these interrogatives can be used with a preposition.

D'où est-ce qu'il vient?	*Where does he come from?*
C'est **pour** quand?	*When do you want it? / When is it for?*
Vous venez **avec** quel train?	*Which train will you be coming on?*
Tu arrives **à** quelle heure?	*What time will you arrive?*

exercise

Which questions would you have asked in order to receive the following replies? Use the *vous* form for 'you' throughout.

E.g. Je mange à midi. → Que faites-vous à midi? → Quand est-ce que vous mangez? → À quelle heure mangez-vous?

a Je vais à la banque.   d Je préfère la robe bleue.
b J'ai trois frères.   e Le film finit à dix heures.
c Il vient du Canada.   f J'aime le foulard jaune.

Interrogative pronouns can be used to find out specific information.

A The interrogative pronouns are as follows:

lequel…? *which (one/ones)…?*	qui…? *who(m)…?*
quoi? *what?*	que…? *what…?*

B **Lequel** agrees in gender and number with the noun it is replacing, in the same way as the relative pronouns **lequel/laquelle/lesquels/lesquelles**. It also combines with **à** and with **de** to form **auquel**, etc. and **duquel**, etc.

J'ai deux robes du soir – laquelle préférez-vous?	*I've got two evening gowns – which do you prefer?*
Je ne sais pas lequel il choisira.	*I don't know which (one) he'll choose.*
Il y a deux spectacles ce soir – auquel veux-tu aller?	*There are two shows tonight – which one do you want to go to?*

C **Qui** can be used as both the subject and the object of a verb, and can appear after a preposition. In direct questions it can be replaced as a subject by **qui est-ce qui** and, as an object, by **qui est-ce que**.

Qui t'a dit ça? / Qui est-ce qui t'a dit ça?	*Who told you that?*
Qui vas-tu aider? / Qui est-ce que tu vas aider?	*Who(m) are you going to help?*

| À qui a-t-il demandé la permission? | Who(m) did he ask for permission? |
| Je n'ai aucune idée qui me l'a donné. | I've no idea who gave it to me. |

D **Que** is used for things or ideas only and can only be the direct object of a verb. It cannot be used with prepositions. It is often replaced by **qu'est-ce qui** and **qu'est-ce que**, mainly in speech.

| Que voulez-vous dire? / Qu'est-ce que vous voulez dire? | What do you mean? |
| Qu'est-ce que c'est? | What's that? / What is it? |

E **Quoi** is used instead of **que** (or **qu'est-ce que**) after a preposition and in indirect questions. It can also be used alone, sometimes as an exclamation.

De quoi est-ce que tu parles?	What are you talking about?
J'ai une nouvelle pour toi. – Quoi?	I've got some news for you. – What?
Quoi?!	What?!

A request for something to be repeated is made by **Comment?** *Pardon?*

exercise

Translate into French.

a *What are you afraid of?*
b *Who works in this office?*
c *What are you saying?*
d *Who is this document for?*

In French a number of patterns are clear in the way numbers (known as cardinal numbers) are formed.

A The numbers 1–16 are single words:

0 zéro	5 cinq	9 neuf	13 treize
1 un(e)	6 six	10 dix	14 quatorze
2 deux	7 sept	11 onze	15 quinze
3 trois	8 huit	12 douze	16 seize
4 quatre			

When used as nouns (*the number 4, he threw a 9*), the numbers 8 and 11 are never elided with the definite article: **le onze, le huit.**

B The numbers 17–19 are compounds based on 10:

17 dix-sept	18 dix-huit	19 dix-neuf

C Between 20 and 60, the multiples of 10 are as follows:

20 vingt   30 trente   40 quarante   50 cinquante   60 soixante

D Numbers between these are compounds, and are hyphenated:

22 vingt-deux	35 trente-cinq	48 quarante-huit

However, compounds that include 1 are formed using **et**:

21 vingt et un(e)   51 cinquante et un(e)   61 soixante et un(e)

E The numbers 70, 80 and 90 are compounds of previous numbers:

70 soixante-dix	80 quatre-vingts*	90 quatre-vingt-dix
71 soixante et onze	81 quatre-vingt-un	91 quatre-vingt-onze
72 soixante-douze	82 quatre-vingt-deux	92 quatre-vingt-douze

*Quatre-vingts standing alone has an **-s**, but this is dropped when a further digit is added.

F The higher numbers are as follows:

100 cent	101 cent un(e)	102 cent deux
200 deux cents	205 deux cent cinq (no -s)	

1 000 mille (invariable, never takes an -s)
1 500 mille cinq cent / quinze cents
1 000 000 un million
3 200 000 trois millions deux cent mille
un milliard *a thousand million / a billion*

Cent and **mille** are not preceded by an indefinite article or *one*, as in English (*a/one hundred, a/one thousand*).

exercise

Write out the following drinks order for the interval at a theatre, inserting the written form of the number shown.

E.g. **12 vins rouges → douze vins rouges**

2 cafés	14 limonades
1 vin blanc	3 panachés *shandy*
12 bières	5 cognacs
7 jus d'orange	

Ordinal numbers are used to express sequence, for example *first*, *second*, *third*, etc. Collective numbers indicate an approximation.

A French ordinal numbers are formed by adding the suffix -ième to the cardinal number.

   3rd (trois) troisième   6th (six) sixième   10th (dix) dixième

- *First* in French has a special form, which must agree in gender with the noun it is referring to.
  1st premier (*m*), première (*f*)
  But when **un** appears in a compound number, the ordinal form is **unième**.
  21st (vingt et un) vingt et unième

- *Second* has two alternative forms in French, the second of which must agree in gender with the noun it is referring to.
  2nd deuxième/second (*m*), seconde (*f*)

- Any number that ends in -e drops this -e in the ordinal form.
  4th (quatre) quatrième   11th (onze) onzième
  12th (douze) douzième

- **Cinq** adds a -u (**cinquième**) and **neuf** changes its -f to a -v (**neuvième**).

- The ordinals **huitième** and **onzième** are never elided with a preceding definite article.
  le huitième jour *the eighth day* la onzième personne *the eleventh person*

B French uses cardinal numbers (not ordinals as in English) in dates.

le neuf juin, le dix-huit octobre	*the ninth of June, the eighteenth of October*

Cardinal numbers are also used with the names of monarchs or popes.

Louis XIV (*spoken:* quatorze)	*Louis XIV (spoken: the Fourteenth)*
le pape Jean-Paul II (*spoken:* deux)	*Pope John Paul II (spoken: the Second)*

However, the ordinal number **premier** is used in both contexts.

le premier septembre	*the first of September*
François I (*spoken:* premier)	*Francis I (spoken: the First)*

C Collective numbers

• To express an approximate number, there are ten nouns that end in **-aine**.

une huitaine *about eight*	une trentaine *about thirty*
une dizaine *about ten*	une quarantaine *about forty*
une douzaine *a dozen*	une cinquantaine *about fifty*
une quinzaine *about fifteen*	une soixantaine *about sixty*
une vingtaine *about twenty*	une centaine *about a hundred*

exercise

See exercise 64 in 'More practice'.

French fractions are formed in a similar way to English fractions but there are some differences in both formation and usage.

A As in English, French fractions consist of a cardinal (*three*, *four*, etc.) plus an ordinal number (*third*, *fourth*, etc.), except for quarters and thirds.

deux sixièmes, trois septièmes	*two sixths, three sevenths*
un quart / trois quarts	*a quarter / three quarters*
un tiers / deux tiers	*a third / two thirds*

In sentences fractions are always preceded by an appropriate article.

Il a perdu les trois quarts de sa fortune.	*He lost three quarters of his fortune.*
J'ai lu un tiers du livre.	*I've read a third of the book.*

B *Half* is expressed using either **demi** or **moitié**, as appropriate:

• **Demi** can be an adjective. It precedes the noun it relates to and is joined to it by a hyphen (and in this position never agrees with it in gender). It may also follow a noun, in which case it is separate and agrees in gender.

une demi-bouteille de whisky	*a half-bottle of whisky*
une demi-heure	*a half-hour*
une bouteille et demie de whisky	*a bottle and a half of whisky*
une heure et demie	*an hour and a half / one and a half hours*

- **Demi** can also be a noun, used only in arithmetic (except for two nouns derived from its use as an adjective: **un demi** *a half (pint/litre of beer) / a glass of beer*, and **la demie** *the half-hour* (on the clock)). In all other uses it is replaced by **la moitié**.

Il a mangé la moitié des biscuits.   *He has eaten half (of the) biscuits.*

C The word **mi-** is like the English word *mid-* or *halfway*. It is invariable and comes before the noun with a hyphen.

Je l'ai rencontré à mi-chemin.   *I met him halfway.*
Il avait les yeux mi-clos.   *His eyes were half closed.*

D In decimal fractions the decimal point is indicated by a comma (**virgule**).

(3,56) trois **virgule** cinquante-six *(3.56) three point five six*

E Proportions are expressed using the preposition **sur**:

Un élève sur dix a réussi.   *One out of ten pupils passed.*

Sept jours sur sept.   *Seven days a week.*
Vingt-quatre heures sur vingt-quatre.   *Twenty-four hours a day.*

exercise

Match up the figures with the appropriate words.

a ⅞ **b** ⅔ **c** ⅓ **d** ¾ **e** 4½ **f** 11/12 **g** 2¾ **h** 8¼

1 deux et trois quarts **2** un tiers **3** quatre et demi **4** deux neuvièmes **5** onze douzièmes **6** sept huitièmes **7** huit et un quart **8** trois quarts

You can use various constructions to give dimensions and distances.

A The most common way to give dimensions is to use the construction **avoir/faire** + (measurement) + **de long/longueur** (*for length*), **de large/largeur** (*for width*), **de haut/hauteur** (*for height*), **de profondeur** (*for depth*), **d'épaisseur** (*for thickness*).

La table a 2 mètres de long. *The table is 2 metres long.*
Les murs faisaient un mètre *The walls were one metre*
d'épaisseur. *thick.*

To give a second dimension (*by*) use **sur**:
La pièce a 5 mètres de long sur *The room is 5 metres long*
4 mètres de large. *by 4 metres wide.*

B You can also use **être** + adjective + **de** + (measurement). The adjectives are **long** (*for length*), **large** (*for width*), **haut** (*for height*), **profond** (*for depth*), **épais** (*for thickness*). Being adjectives, these must agree with the noun.

Ce chemin est long de 2 *This path is 2 kilometres*
kilomètres. *long.*
La pièce est longue de 3 mètres. *The room is 3 metres long.*
L'eau est profonde de 20 mètres. *The water is 20 metres*
deep.

If you wish to give a second dimension simply use **et**:
La tour est haute de 15 mètres *The tower is 15 metres*
et large de 4 mètres. *high and 4 metres wide.*

C To ask about dimensions use one of the following questions.

Quelle est la longeur/largeur (etc.) de…?	*What is the length/width (etc.) of…?*
(Cette pièce) a/fait combien de long/large (etc.)?	*How long/wide (etc.) is (this room)?*
(Cette pièce) est longue/large (etc.) de combien?	*How long/wide (etc.) is (this room)?*

D To say how far away something is (in distance or time), use the preposition **à**.

On est à un kilomètre de la gare.	*We're one kilometre away from the train station.*
L'hôpital est à 5 minutes d'ici.	*The hospital is 5 minutes from here.*
Le centre commercial est à combien d'ici?	*How far is the shopping centre from here?*

exercise

Give the dimensions of the following monuments using the *avoir* construction.

E.g. L'arc de Triomphe *a 50 mètres de haut.*

a *50m high, 45m wide*

b *300m high*

la tour Eiffel

c *80m high*

le Sacré-Cœur

In French as in English the 12-hour and the 24-hour clocks are both used.

A When saying the time, you use the word **heure(s)** *hour(s)*, except for midday and midnight. To ask the time you say **Quelle heure est-il?**

Times on the hour

Il est une heure / cinq heures.	*It's one o'clock / five o'clock.*
Il est midi.	*It's midday / noon / twelve o'clock.*
Il est minuit.	*It's midnight/twelve o'clock.*

B For times between the hours, minutes are given after the hour:

* *Half past* is **et demie**, except with **midi** and **minuit** when it is **et demi**

Il est six heures et demie.	*It's half past six.*
Il est midi et demi.	*It's half past twelve (noon).*

* *Quarter past* is **et quart**, and *quarter to* **moins le quart**

Je pars à huit heures et quart.	*I leave at quarter past eight.*
Il arrive à neuf heures moins le quart.	*He arrives at quarter to nine.*

* Minutes past the hour are added directly after the hour

Il est trois heures vingt.	*It's twenty past three.*

* Minutes to the hour are expressed by using **moins**

Il est onze heures moins cinq.	*It's five to eleven.*

C Times of the day using the 12-hour clock are indicated by **de**…

Il est dix heures du matin / du soir.	*It's ten o'clock in the morning/ evening.*
Il est trois heures de l'après-midi.	*It's three o'clock in the afternoon.*

To indicate the time something happened use **à** (or **vers** for approximate times).

Elle est partie à cinq heures.	*She left at five o'clock.*
Je vais arriver vers quatre heures.	*I'll arrive at about four o'clock.*

To express the idea of *between* two times you say **de … à**, or **entre … et**.

Je serai là de dix heures à midi.	*I'll be there from ten o'clock to midday.*
Je serai au bureau entre dix heures et midi.	*I'll be at the office between ten o'clock and midday.*

D The 24-hour clock is used more widely in French than in English. It works the same way in French except that the word **heure(s)** is included.

08h15 huit heures quinze	*08.15 eight fifteen*
20h45 vingt heures quarante-cinq	*20.45 twenty forty-five*

exercise

See exercises 67 and 68 in 'More practice'.

There are some difference in the way that days, dates and years are used in French.

A

Les jours de la semaine	
lundi	*Monday*
mardi	*Tuesday*
mercredi	*Wednesday*
jeudi	*Thursday*
vendredi	*Friday*
samedi	*Saturday*
dimanche	*Sunday*

Les mois de l'année			
janvier	*January*	juillet	*July*
février	*February*	août	*August*
mars	*March*	septembre	*September*
avril	*April*	octobre	*October*
mai	*May*	novembre	*November*
juin	*June*	décembre	*December*

These are all written without capitals.

B Dates of the month are expressed using cardinal numbers.
le trente décembre   *the thirtieth of December*
vendredi, le quinze août / le vendredi, quinze août *Friday, 15 August*

The exception is **premier** *first*, as in **le premier mai** *the first of May*.

C The day on which something regularly occurs is given using the definite article, whereas one particular day is given without it.

Je vais à la piscine le samedi.   *I go to the swimming pool on Saturdays.*

Je vais à la piscine samedi.   *I'm going to the swimming
                                       pool on Saturday.*

D **En** is used to mean *in* with months or years (also **au mois
de** for months).
 en avril *in April*   en 1988 *in 1988*
 au mois de janvier *in January*

E **En** is also used with the seasons, with the exception of spring
where **au** is used.
 au printemps *in spring*   en automne *in autumn*
 en été *in summer*   en hiver *in winter*

F The year can be given in two ways.
 en 1999 = en mil neuf cent quatre-vingt-dix-neuf
           en dix-neuf cent quatre-vingt-dix-neuf

G The following phrases are used when talking about days and
dates.
 Quel jour / Quelle date sommes- *What day/date is it?*
  nous?
 On est quel jour / quelle date? *What day/date is it?*
 Quelle est la date?   *What's the date?*
 C'est / On est jeudi, le 15 août. *It's Thursday, 15 August.*

exercise

See exercise 69 in 'More practice'.

Depuis, il y a and ***venir de*** generally combine with tenses in ways that are different from English.

A Depuis

• **Depuis** + present tense means *have been ... for/since*, and describes an action which continues into the present.

Je travaille ici depuis deux ans.	*I've been working here for two years.*
Je suis ici depuis lundi.	*I've been here since Monday.*

• **Depuis** + imperfect tense means *had been ... for/since*, and describes an action clearly in the past.

Elle le connaissait depuis dix ans.	*She had known him for ten years.*

Note: In the negative you use the perfect and pluperfect tenses, as in English.

Il n'a pas travaillé depuis des années.	*He hasn't worked for years.*
Il n'était pas venu depuis longtemps.	*He hadn't been for a long time.*

• When **depuis** is followed by a second verb and subject, you use **que**.

Elle travaille ici depuis que vous êtes arrivé.	*She's worked here since you arrived.*

B **Il y a** with expressions of time

• **Il y a** (present tense) + a verb in an appropriate tense
means *ago*.

Je suis arrivé il y a trois semaines. *I arrived three weeks ago.*
Il y a cinq ans je travaillais. *Five years ago I was working.*

• **Il y a,** like **depuis,** is also used to indicate the duration of
time for something still continuing (*have been ... for*). To
indicate this you use **il y a** (present tense) + the period of
time + **que** followed by a clause in the present tense. **Voilà
que** and **ça fait que** are used in the same way.

Il y a dix ans que je le connais. *I've known him for ten years.*

Voilà / Ça fait dix ans que je le *I've known him for ten years.*
connais.

• When **il y a ... que** and **ça fait ... que** are used with the
same structure, but in the imperfect tense, they translate
the English *had been ... for*.

Il y avait / Ça faisait dix mois *I had known him for ten months.*
que je le connaissais.

C **Venir de** expresses the English *has just* (when used in the
present tense) or *had just* (when used in the imperfect tense).

Ils viennent de quitter le bureau. *They've just left the office.*
Elle venait d'arriver. *She had just arrived.*

exercise

See exercises 70 and 71 in 'More practice'.

Il y a can mean either there is or there are.

A Look at the following sentences:

Il y a une boisson dans le frigo. *There is a drink in the fridge*

Il y a des dossiers sur mon . *There are some files on my*
bureau *desk.*

As these sentences show, **il y a** is used only in the singular, whether the following noun is singular or plural. In negative statements, **ne … pas** enclose the pronoun y and the conjugated verb **a**.

Il n'y a pas de place. *There's no room.*

B Il y a can also be used this way in past and future tenses.

• Imperfect tense (*there was/were*):

Il y avait beaucoup de monde *There were a lot of people*
au match. *at the match.*

Puis il y avait une discussion. *Then there was a discussion.*

Il y avait une fois… *Once upon a time…* (lit.
There was once…)

• Perfect tense (*there has / have been; there was / were*):

Il y a eu un accident! *There has been an accident!*

Il y a eu des problèmes. *There have been / There were*
problems.

Il n'y a pas eu de problèmes. *There haven't been any*
problems.

Note: The past participle **eu** does not agree with any preceding direct object.

Tous les problèmes qu'il y a eu ont été facilement résolus.	*All the problems there were have been easily resolved.*

- Future tense (*there will be*):

Il y aura un grand repas après l'exposition.	*There will be a big meal after the exhibition.*
Il y aura des feux d'artifice après le repas.	*There will be fireworks after the meal.*

C A slightly more formal alternative to **il y a** is **il existe**, also used in the singular only:

Il existe deux cinémas en ville.	*There are two cinemas in town.*

D You can use **il reste** to say *there is/are* left:

Il reste du fromage?	*Is there any cheese left?*

exercise

Match the correct English translation to a French sentence from the box.

E.g. **Il y a une boisson sur la table.** There was a drink on the table. There is a drink on the table. ✓

a There has been an accident.
b There will be an accident.

c There will be three people.
d There were three people.

e There's not much to see.
f There wasn't much to see.

> 1 Il y a eu un accident.
> 2 Il y avait trois personnes.
> 3 Il n'y a pas grand chose à voir.

In French, there are two words for *yes*, *oui* and *si*. *No* is translated as *non*.

A In most situations, **oui** is used to mean *yes*.

Tu viens avec nous? Oui.	*Are you coming with us? Yes, I am. / Yes, I'm coming.* etc.

The above response shows that English can sometimes use longer replies than are necessary in French.

Si is needed to answer a negative question, or to contradict a negative statement. **Si** can stand alone for the long English contradiction forms shown here.

Vous ne l'avez pas vu? Si (je l'ai vu).	*Didn't you see him? Yes I did (see him).*
Vous ne le ferez jamais. Mais si!	*You will never do it. Oh yes I will!*

B The English word *no* is translated by **non** (or **mais non** in more exclamatory uses). Often a polite refusal can be given by using **merci** alone. Again, English often uses a longer answer.

Je peux vous offrir un cognac? Merci.	*Would you like a brandy? No, thank you.*
Vous voulez un café? Non, merci.	*Would you like a coffee? No thanks.*
Il va pleuvoir? Non.	*Will it rain? No (it won't).*
Vous êtes venu tout seul? Mais non, je suis avec ma femme!	*Did you come alone? No, I'm with my wife!*

C The word **que** must be added before **oui, si** and **non** when used after **peut-être** *perhaps*, **espérer** *to hope* and verbs of saying and thinking.

Est-ce que tu peux venir? J'ai déjà dit que oui.	*Can you come? I've already said I can.*
Il a reçu ta lettre? J'espère que oui.	*Did he receive your letter? I hope so.*
Il n'arrivera pas aujourd'hui. Je crois que si.	*He will not arrive today. I think he will.*
Vont-ils être en retard? J'espère que non.	*Are they going to be late? I hope not.*
Il est déjà parti? Je crois que non.	*Has he already left? I don't think so.*
Il va pleuvoir? Peut-être que oui, peut-être que non.	*Will it rain? Perhaps it will, perhaps it won't.*

exercise

Read the following questions and choose either 1 or 2 as an appropriate response.

E.g. Il est déjà midi?	1 Oui. ✓
	2 Si.
a Tu vas venir?	1 Oui, bien sûr!
	2 Mais si!
b Vous n'avez pas écrit la lettre.	1 Si, je l'ai écrite.
	2 Oui, j'ai écrit la lettre.
c Elle ne parle pas français.	1 Oui, elle parle français.
	2 Si, elle parle français.
d Il est déjà arrivé?	1 Mais si!
	2 Oui, il est arrivé ce matin.

It is important to know the gender of countries and the rules governing the use of related adjectives and nouns.

A Most countries are feminine; these end in a consonant plus -e or -ie.

la France *France*	l'Angleterre *England*	la Russie *Russia*
la Norvège *Norway*	l'Espagne *Spain*	l'Italie *Italy*
la Pologne *Poland*	l'Allemagne *Germany*	

- Others are masculine.

le Japon Japan	le Canada *Canada*
le Portugal *Portugal*	le Mexique *Mexico*.

- A few are plural, as they are in English.
  les États-Unis *the United States* les Caraïbes *the West Indies*

B The definite article (**le, la, les**) is used before names of countries.

Le Maroc est un pays très *Morocco is a very interesting*
intéressant. *country.*

- To say *to* or *in* a country, use **en** for feminine countries, **au** for masculine countries and **aux** for plural countries.
  Nous allons en France, puis au *We are going to France,*
  Luxembourg et puis aux *then to Luxembourg and*
  Pays-Bas. *then to the Netherlands.*

- To say *from* a country, use **de** for feminine countries, **du** for masculine countries and **des** for plurals countries.
  Il est arrivé d'Allemagne ce *He arrived from Germany*
  matin. *this morning.*

Il vient du Canada. *He comes from Canada.*

C French *adjectives* of nationality are not written with a capital letter.

C'est une voiture italienne. *It's an Italian car.*
Ils sont canadiens. *They are Canadian.*

- When using *nouns* of nationality the usual rules of adjectival agreement apply, but the nationality is written with a capital letter.

C'est une Danoise / une *She's a Dane / a*
Française. *Frenchwoman.*

D When referring to the language, use the masculine noun without a capital. If there is an adverb or other qualifier, insert the masculine definite article.

Parlez-vous français? *Do you speak French?*
Tu parles très bien le russe. *You speak Russian very well.*

exercise

Give the gender of the following countries.

a Argentine   f Russie
b Corse   g Pérou
c Suisse   h Mexique
d Hongrie   i Thaïlande
e Maroc   j Tibet

You need inversion after direct speech and after certain expressions. it can also be used for questions.

A When expressing *she said, I exclaimed, he replied,* etc. after direct speech, the subject and the verb are inverted (reversed).

« C'est ridicule », dit-il.   *'It's ridiculous', he says.*

« Bonjour », a répondu Pauline.   *'Hello', replied Pauline.*

When the third-person singular of the verb ends in a vowel, a -t- is inserted after the verb and before the subject pronoun **il**, **elle** or **on**.

« C'est combien? » demande-t-elle. *'How much is it?' she asks.*

« Bonjour », a-t-il dit.   *'Hello', he said.*

• Any object and reflexive pronouns precede the finite verb.

« La météo est bonne », nous a-t-il dit.   *'The forecast is good', he told us.*

« Bonjour! », s'exclama-t-elle.   *'Hello!', she exclaimed.*

• If the verb of saying comes first, word order is normal.

Elle m'a dit, « Bonjour ».   *She said 'Hello' to me.*

B The subject and verb are also inverted after the following, when they begin the sentence.

à peine … que *scarcely*	encore *nevertheless*
ainsi *thus*	peut-être *perhaps*
aussi *therefore* (not when meaning *also, as well*)	sans doute *doubtless, no doubt*

Peut-être a-t-elle changé d'avis.	*Perhaps she has changed her mind.*
Ainsi l'avocat a-t-il décidé de quitter son travail.	*And so the lawyer decided to give up his job.*
Sans doute va-t-elle passer la nuit chez des amis.	*No doubt she is going to spend the night with friends.*
Je suis fatigué, aussi ai-je besoin de dormir.	*I am tired, therefore/ consequently I need to sleep.*

Peut-être and **sans doute** can be followed by **que**, without inversion.

Peut-être que tu le verras vendredi. *Perhaps you'll see him on Friday.*

C Remember that one way to ask questions in French is to invert the subject and verb.

| Avez-vous promis? | *Did you promise?* |
| Est-elle à la réunion? | *Is she in the meeting?* |

exercise

Rewrite the following as questions, using inversion.

E.g. Il a parlé au médecin. → A-t-il parlé au médecin?

a Il a expliqué le projet.
b Elles sont arrivées à l'heure.
c Elle vous a téléphoné ce matin.

These are words that are similar to English words, but which have a different meaning to that which you might expect.

Faux amis literally means *false friends*. The following table gives some examples, followed by a translation into English. It then gives the English word that is similar to the French word, along with its translation back into French.

False friend	Meaning	English	French
actuellement	*at the present time, currently*	*actually*	en fait, à vrai dire, vraiment
assister à	*to be present at, to attend*	*to assist*	aider
l'avis (*nm*)	*notice, option; opinion*	*advice*	le conseil
la banque	*the bank* (for money)	*bank, riverbank*	la rive, le bord de la rivière
la chance	usual use *(good) luck*	*chance*	le hasard
fameux	*notorious*	*famous*	célèbre
l'humeur (*nf*)	*mood*	*humour*	l'humour (*nm*)
la journée	*day(time)*	*journey*	le voyage, le trajet
la librairie	*bookshop*	*library*	la bibliothèque
la monnaie	*currency; small change*	*money*	l'argent (*nm*)
la nouvelle	*piece of news*	*novel*	le roman
passer un examen	*to sit an exam*	*to pass an exam*	réussir à un examen
la pièce	*room; coin; play* (theatre)	*piece*	le morceau

la place	*public square, seat, job.*	*place*	l'endroit (*nm*), le lieu
rester	*to remain, stay*	*to rest*	se reposer
le spectacle	*show, sight*	*spectacles*	les lunettes (*nf*)
user	*to wear out, wear thin*	*to use*	utiliser, se servir de, employer

Some words have two meanings, only one of which is close to the English.

l'histoire   *history/story*
une balle   *ball* (e.g. for tennis)/*bullet*
la campagne   *countryside/(military)*
campaign
les parents   *parents/relatives*

exercise

Translate the following sentences into French.

E.g.   *Have you got any change?* → Tu as de la monnaie?

a *I am going to the library to choose some books.*

b *Where are my spectacles?*

c *The journey lasted* (**durer**) *twenty-four hours.*

d *She's a very famous woman.*

e *It's a very interesting place.*

f *Pass me a piece of bread please.*

g *They're going to attend the meeting tomorrow.*

Expressions of quantity include terms like *a lot of*, *several*, *most of*, or *a packet of*.

A Several expressions of quantity are followed by **de**.

Il vend beaucoup de voitures.	*He sells lots of cars.*
Il y a un certain nombre de lettres.	*There are quite a few letters.*
Il y a tant de choses à voir.	*There are so many things to see.*
Il y a énormément d'enfants ici.	*There are loads of children here.*

assez de *enough*

autant de *as much, as many*

beaucoup de *much, many, a lot, lots*

combien de … ? *how much? how many?*

énormément de *loads, an enormous amount*

moins de *less, fewer*

peu de / un peu de *little / a little*

plus de *more*

tant de *so much, so many*

trop de *too much,*

un certain nombre de *quite a few, a certain number*

B Nouns expressing quantity are also followed by **de**.

Vous prenez 200 grammes de champignons?	*Would you like 200 grammes of mushrooms?*
J'ai une bouteille d'eau minérale.	*I've got a bottle of mineral water.*

Je voudrais trois tranches de jambon.	*I'd like three slices of ham.*

C After **la plupart**, **de** combines with the definite article (**le, la, les**). The verb agrees in number with the noun following **la plupart de**.

La plupart de la collection a été perdue.	*Most of the collection was lost.*
La plupart des clients sont très contents.	*Most of the customers are very happy.*

D Some indefinite adjectives indicate quantity or number. As they are adjectives they do not require **de**.

Il y a **quelques** pots de yaourt dans le frigo.	*There are a few pots of yoghurt in the fridge.*
Il y a **plusieurs** boîtes de sardines dans le placard.	*There are several tins of sardines in the cupboard.*
Certains clients demandent un remboursement.	*Some customers are asking for a refund.*

exercise

Translate the following into French.

E.g. *two kilos of flour* → **deux kilos de farine**

a *a bottle of mineral water*   d *a tin of peaches*
b *a kilo of apples*   e *a cup of tea*
c *a packet of biscuits*

Verbs followed by *à* + infinitive

aider à	*to help to*	se mettre à	*to start to*
s'amuser à	*to amuse oneself at*	obliger à	*to oblige to*
apprendre à	*to learn to*	parvenir à	*to succeed in*
arriver à	*to manage to*	penser à	*to think of*
s'attendre à	*to expect to*	persister à	*to persist in*
autoriser à	*to authorize to*	pousser à	*to push to*
chercher à	*to try to*	se préparer à	*to prepare oneself to*
commencer à	*to start to*		
consentir à	*to consent to*	renoncer à	*to renounce something*
consister à	*to consist of*		
continuer à	*to continue to*	réussir à	*to succeed in*
se décider à	*to decide to*	rester à	*to be left to*
demander à	*to ask to*	servir à	*to be used for*
encourager à	*to encourage to*		
forcer à	*to force to*	tarder à	*to delay (doing), be late in*
hésiter à	*to hesitate to*		
s'intéresser à	*to be interested in*	tenir à	*to be keen on*
inviter à	*to invite to*		

Verbs followed by *de* + infinitive

accepter de	*to accept to*	avoir besoin de	*to need to*
(s')arrêter de	*to stop doing*	cesser de	*to stop*

conseiller de	to *advise* to	permettre de	to *allow* to
craindre de	to *fear doing*	persuader de	to *persuade* to
décider de	to *decide* to	promettre de	to *promise* to
défendre de	to *forbid* to	proposer de	to *suggest* to
demander de	to *ask s.o.* to	rappeler de	to *remind*
dire de	to *tell* to	se rappeler de	to *remember*
empêcher de	to *prevent from*	recommander de	to *recommend* to
essayer de	to *try* to		
éviter de	to *avoid doing*	refuser de	to *refuse* to
finir de	to *finish doing*	regretter de	to *regret doing*
interdire de	to *forbid* to	remercier to	to *thank for*
s'occuper de	to *deal with*	se souvenir de	to *remember doing*
offrir de	to *offer* to		
ordonner de	to *order* to	suggérer de	to *suggest doing*

Unit 1: a le **b** la **c** l' **d** la **e** le **f** l' **g** le **h** le

Unit 2: a un **b** une **c** un **d** une **e** un **f** un

Unit 3: a le **b** les **c** la **d** le **e** le, le

Unit 4: a le **b** la **c** le **d** la

Unit 5: a la **b** le **c** le **d** la **e** la **f** l' (*f*)

Unit 6: a le **b** la **c** le, la **d** la

Unit 8: a Il est; C'est **b** est-il; il est **c** Ce sont **d** C'est

Unit 9: des champignons; des oeufs; du pain; de la confiture; du lait; du fromage; du poisson; de la soupe

Unit 10: a après **b** contre **c** dans **d** chez; avec

Unit 12: a par **b** parmi **c** pour **d** vers **e** par

Unit 13: a du **b** de **c** de **d** de l' **e** de

Unit 14: a Il a mal à la main. **b** Elle a mal aux dents. **c** Il a mal au pied.

Unit 15: a 2 **b** 4 **c** 3 **d** 5 **e** 1

Unit 17: a courts; verts **b** méchant; timide

Unit 18: a finale **b** vieux; gentil **c** frais **d** nouvel

Unit 19: a bière française **b** vieil ordinateur **c** Tous les documents; nouveau bureau **d** bonne histoire amusante

Unit 20: a 2 **b** 4 **c** 5 **d** 6 **e** 3 **f** 1

Unit 21: a joyeusement **b** vraiment **c** poliment
d résolument **e** parfaitement **f** profondément

Unit 22: a bas **b** cher **c** mieux **d** bien **e** bien/mal
f haut **g** fort **h** net

Unit 25: a 4 **b** 1 **c** 2 **d** 3

Unit 27: a mieux; le mieux **b** plus mal; le plus mal

Unit 28: a plusieurs **b** Tous **c** certaines

Unit 29: a Quelqu'un **b** Chacun **c** Personne **d** Chaque
e quelques-unes **f** quelque chose

Unit 30: a 3 **b** 1 **c** 4 **d** 2

Unit 31: a porte **b** écoutent **c** prépare **d** cherches

Unit 32: a appelle **b** nageons **c** essaient **d** manges
e achète

Unit 33: 1a obéit **b** applaudissent **c** réussissons
d finit **e** ouvrez **f** souffrent **2a** Elle ouvre le cadeau.
b Il choisit un stylo. **c** Tout le monde applaudit. **d** Ils
remplissent les bouteilles.

Unit 34: a j'attends, ils attendent **b** vous vendez, elle vend
c tu entends, elles entendent **d** ils perdent, nous perdons
e nous descendons, il descend

Unit 35: a Il se lève à dept heures. **b** Elles se brossent les dents **c** Nous nous couchons à onze heures. **d** Je me lave les cheveux.

Unit 37: a On va en France à Pâques. **b** On mange à huit heures. **c** On se rencontre demain? **d** Quelquefois on préfère le cinéma au théâtre.

Unit 38: a Moi, je préfère le vin rouge. **b** Lui, il travaille ici, pas moi. **c** Elle? Elle a mal à la tête. **d** Moi, je vais avec eux.

Unit 39: a les tiens **b** les miennes **c** les vôtres

Unit 40: a C'est celui de ma sœur. **b** Ce sont ceux de mon collègue. **c** C'est celle de mon père.

Unit 41: a que **b** qui **c** qui

Unit 43: a laquelle **b** auxquelles

Unit 44: a tout ce que **b** tout ce qui **c** tout ce qu' **d** tout ce qu' **e** tout ce qu'

Unit 48: a Tu as/Vous avez tort **b** Il a peur. **c** Tu as/Vous avez une nouvelle voiture. **d** J'ai faim. **e** Ils ont/Elles ont de la chance. **f** Elle a un rendez-vous. **g** Ils ont trois filles. **h** Nous avons une maison secondaire.

Unit 49: 1a je b ils/elles c nous d il e tu 2a Il a 10 ans. b Je suis ingénieur. c J'ai faim. d Ils sont espagnols. Elles sont espagnoles. e Tu as/Vous avez raison. f Elle est heureuse. g Tu as/Vous avez/As-tu/Avez-vous soif? h Elle est jolie.

Unit 51: a Apprenez-vous/Vous apprenez l'anglais? b Je vais prendre une tasse de thé. c Elle prend une douche. d Il proment un bon repas. e Je vais mettre mon manteau.

Unit 52: a Elle vent aller à la banque. b Tu peux/Vous pouvez manger maintenant. c Il veut acheter un vélo. d Je voudrais un kilo de pommes. e Nous pouvons/On peut entrer maintenant.

Unit 53: a Je dois aller à Paris. b Il doit être dans le salon. c Elle doit téléphoner à Rouen. d Nous savons faire du ski. e Ils doivent promettre. f Je connais bien Saumur.

Unit 54: a veulent b devons c nous promenons d veulent

Unit 56: a Va; Allez b aie; ayez c Mets; Mettez d Prends/Prenez

Unit 60: a visité b mangé c admiré d acheté e rencontré

Unit 61: a Elle est sortie de la gare.   **b** Ils/Elles sont sorties du cinéma.   **c** Elle est tombée du vélo/de la bicyclette.
d Il est entré dans la banque.   **e** Elle est née le quatre janvier.

Unit 62: a Tu t'es reposé(e)   **b** Ils se sont arrêtés   **c** Nous nous sommes assis(es)   **d** Vous vous êtes dépêché(e)(s)(es)
e Elle s'est ennuyée

Unit 63: a achetées   **b** utilisé   **c** lavés   **d** reçue

Unit 64: a prenaient   **b** finissiez   **c** jouais   **d** couchais
e travaillais   **f** rentraient

Unit 65: a lisais; a sonné   **b** écoutait; a frappé   **c** faisions;
ai perdu

Unit 66: a avait   **b** était   **c** étais   **d** avaient   **e** avais
f étions

Unit 67: a ont frappé   **b** a attendu   **c** j'ai choisi
d a perdu   **e** a fini   **f** ont répondu

Unit 68: a fera   **b** louera   **c** écrira   **d** achètera
e visitera   **f** téléphonera

Unit 69: a 3   **b** 1   **c** 2   **d** 5   **e** 4

Unit 70: a il aurait   **b** je devrais   **c** nous prendrions
d vous pourriez   **e** tu voudrais   **f** elle finirait   **g** je serais
h elles feraient   **i** vous achèteriez   **j** il viendrait

Unit 72: a avais travaillé; aurais fait **b** avais, achèterais **c** finis; pourrai

Unit 73: a Après avoir appris **b** Après être arrivé **c** Après m'être reposé(e) **d** Après être arrivé(e)s

Unit 75: a je veuille; vous vouliez **b** j'aille; vous alliez **c** je sache, vous sachiez **d** je vienne; vous veniez **e** je boive; vous buviez **f** je sois; vous soyez

Unit 76: a qu'il ait gagné le prix. **b** qu'elle ait appris à conduire. **c** que tu te sois reposé(e) un peu. **d** que vous ayez passé le weekend chez eux. **e** qu'elles soient allées en vacances. **f** qu'il soit parti à l'heure. **g** que vous ayez parlé au curé.

Unit 78: a Il est important qu'il fasse ses devoirs **b** Il faut que vous travailliez. **c** Il est impossible qu'il réussisse.

Unit 80: a au contraire; *Me, I like it, but she on the other hand/contrary doesn't like it at all.* **b** donc; *It was snowing so I didn't go.* **c** mais; *He wanted to come with us but he didn't have the time.* **d** puis; *He did the cooking then I washed up.* **e** ainsi; *He repaired it so/and so we were able to leave.* **f** d'ailleurs; *I don't want to buy it, besides I haven't got enough money.*

Unit 81: Comme; Pendant que; qu'; ou … ou; Donc; s'; aussitôt que

Unit 83: a Non, il ne l'a pas vu. **b** Non, je ne suis pas parti avant minuit. **c** Non, il ne sera pas arrivé à l'heure. **d** Non, elle ne s'est pas maquillée avant de sortir.

Unit 84: a Tu achètes un ordinateur? Est-ce que tu achètes un ordinateur? Achètes-tu un ordinateur? **b** Il est pharmacien? Est-ce qu'il est pharmacien? Est-il pharmacien? **c** Elle adore le théâtre? Est-ce qu'elle adore le théâtre? Adore-t-elle le théâtre? **d** Vous aimez le vin? Est-ce que vous aimez le vin? Aimez-vous le vin? **e** Ils vont en ville? Est-ce qu'ils vont en ville? Vont-ils en ville?

Unit 85: a Vous allez où?/Où est-ce que vous allez? Où allez-vous? **b** Vous avez combien de frères? Combien de frères est-ce que vous avez? Combien de frères avez-vous? **c** Il vient d'où? D'où est-ce qu'il vient? D'où vient-il? **d** Vous préférez quelle robe? Quelle robe est-ce que vous préférez? Quelle robe préférez-vous? **e** Le film finit à quelle heure? A quelle heure est-ce que le film finit? A quelle heure finit le film? **f** Vous aimez quel foulard? Quel foulard est-ce que vous aimez? Quel foulard aimez-vous?

Unit 86: a De quoi as-tu/avez-vous peur? **b** Lequel des ordinateurs veux-tu/voulez-vous? **c** Qui travaille dans ce bureau? **d** Qu'est-ce que tu dis/vous dites? Que dis-tu/dites-vous?

Unit 87: deux cafés; un vin blanc; douze bières; sept jus d'orange; quatorze limonades; trois panachés; cinq cognacs

Unit 89: a 6 **b** 4 **c** 2 **d** 8 **e** 3 **f** 5 **g** 1 **h** 7

Unit 90: a L'arc de Triomphe a 50m de haute/hauteur sur 45m de large/de largeur. **b** La tour Eiffel a 300m de haut/de hauteur. **c** La basilique du Sacré-Coeur a 80m de haut/de hauteur.

Unit 94: a 1 **b** 2 **c** 3

Unit 95: a 1 **b** 1 **c** 2 **d** 2

Unit 96: a f **b** f **c** f **d** f **e** m **f** f **g** m **h** m **i** f **j** m

Unit 97: a A-t-il expliqué …? **b** Sont-elles arrivées …? **c** Vous a-t-elle téléphoné …?

Unit 98: a Je vais à la bibliothèque choisir des livres. **b** Où sont mes lunettes? **c** Le voyage/trajet a duré vingt-quatre heures. **d** C'est une femme très renommée. **e** C'est un endroit/lieu très intéressant. **f** Passe-moi/Passez-moi un morceau de pain, s'il te/vous plaît. **g** Ils vont assister à la réunion demain.

Unit 99: a une bouteille d'eau minérale **b** un kilo de pommes **c** un paquet de biscuits **d** une boîte de pêches **e** une tasse de thé

Exercise 1 (Unit 1)

Spot the nouns and their genders in the following wordsearch grid. The nouns in the grid are in the box beside it.

```
l e v i n o s t f m
p t l m y r l n y p
s l e l a i t q r b
l a c h e m i s e t
i r h f l e p l a n
m a i l a c r è m e
a d e e l' h o m m e
g i n p v x a n l n
e o c r p l a r u e
o l a v o i t u r e
```

rue	crème
chemise	vin
plan	lait
homme	voiture
chien	radio
image	

Exercise 2 (Unit 1)

Give the plural forms of these singular nouns, remembering to include the plural of the definite article as well.

E.g. bras → les bras

a journal *newspaper*

b banque *bank*

c voix *voice*

d fromage *cheese*

e bateau *boat*

f cinéma *cinema*

Exercise 3 (Unit 2)

Complete the following dialogues using *un*, *une* or *des*, *de* or *d'*.

E.g. Il y a _____ supermarché par ici, s'il vous plaît? →
　　Il y a *un* supermarché par ici, s'il vous plaît?

a Vous avez _____ stylo, s'il vous plaît?
　Oui, il y a (*there are*) _____ stylos dans mon bureau.
b Je peux avoir _____ boisson?
　Oui, il y a _____ boissons dans le frigo.
c Vous avez _____ pommes?
　Non, je n'ai pas _____ pommes, mais j'ai _____ bananes
　et _____ oranges.

Exercise 4 (Unit 5)

**What are the following in French? Use *un*, *une* or *des* as
appropriate in your answer. Refer to earlier units if necessary.**

a *a foot*　　　　　　　　f *television sets*
b *an arm*　　　　　　　 g *lamps*
c *a nose*　　　　　　　　h *a cinema*
d *a horse*　　　　　　　 i *a church*
e *a book*　　　　　　　　j *a female doctor*

Exercise 5 (Unit 7)

Form singular nouns from the following plurals.

E.g. les grands-mères (*grandmothers*) → la grand-mère
a les beaux-pères *fathers-in-law*
b les haut-parleurs *loudspeakers*

c les porte-clefs *keyrings*

d les chefs d'œuvre *masterpieces*

e les rouges-gorges *robins*

f les oiseaux-mouches *humming birds*

Exercise 6 (Unit 8)

Match the sentences to each other.

E.g. Il est sept heures. → *It's seven o'clock.*

1 C'est mon bureau.   a *It's nine o'clock.*

2 Il est neuf heures.   b *Who's that?*

3 Il est facile de faire cela.   c *They're lilacs.*

4 Ce sont des lilas.   d *It's true that it's late.*

5 Il est vrai qu'il est tard.   e *It's my office/desk.*

6 Qui est-ce?   f *It's easy to do that.*

Exercise 7 (Unit 11)

Complete the following with appropriate prepositions using the English as a guide.

E.g. Elle est _____ ville. *She is in town.* → Elle est *en* ville.

a La librairie est _____ la poste et la boulangerie. *The bookshop is between the post office and the bakery.*

b _____ la pluie, ils sont sortis. *In spite of the rain they went out.*

c Il est mort _____ 1982. *He died in 1982.*

d Je suis allé _____ France pour la première fois _____ 1992. *I went to France for the first time in 1992.*

e Cette chaise est _____ métal – l'autre est _____ bois.
   This chair is in metal – the other is in wood.

Exercise 8 (Unit 13)

Translate the following sentences into French.

E.g. *These are the hotel keys.* → Ce sont les clés de l'hôtel.

a *Here's Hélène's case.* (**la valise**)
b *It's Jean's flat.*
c *The train arrives at six in the evening.*
d *I like the colour of the bikes.*

Exercise 9 (Unit 14)

**How many sentences can you make from the following table?
Translate all those you find.**

Pierre va	à	pâtisserie (*nf*)
Nous allons	à la	école (*nf*)
Je travaille	au	cinéma (*nm*)
Mes enfants vont	à l'	pharmacie (*nf*)
On achète des gâteaux	aux	magasins (*nmpl*)
Elle va		église (*nf*)
Vous travaillez		café (*nm*)
Je vais		Montpellier

Exercise 10 (Unit 16)

Complete the following sentences using the appropriate possessive adjectives.

E.g. _____ clé est dans ma poche. → *Ma* clé est dans ma poche.

a Dans _____ valise, Maurice a _____ vêtements (*nmpl*), _____ affaires de toilette (*nfpl*) et _____ permis de conduire (*nm*).

b Quand elle part en vacances elle prend toujours _____ raquette (*nf*) et _____ chaussures (*nfpl*) de tennis.

c Vous avez _____ passeport?

d Tu as passé _____ vacances (*nfpl*) en Italie?

e Jeanne est arrivée portant _____ nouvelle robe (*nf*).

f Ils veulent _____ journaux? Ils sont sur la table.

g Nous avons acheté des fleurs pour _____ grand-mère.

h Il a envoyé un courrier électronique à _____ collègues (*nmpl*).

Exercise 11 (Unit 17)

Complete the following conversations with the appropriate form of the adjectives in brackets.

E.g. Vous avez les documents (récent)? → Vous avez les documents *récents*?

a Simone Vous avez les tasses (blanc) (*nfpl*)?

   Danielle Non. Elles sont sur la (petit) table dans le salon.

b Paul   C'est un (bon) hôtel.
  Jean   Oui. Mais ma chambre est (cher).
  Paul   Mais elle est (grand).
c Henri   Mon amie (espagnol) arrive aujourd'hui.
  Hélène Comment est-elle?
  Henri   Elle est très (joli). Elle a les cheveux (*nmpl*) (long)
         et (noir). Et les yeux (brun).

Exercise 12 (Unit 18)

Complete the following sentences using the adjectives in brackets.

E.g. **C'est une (vieux) amie. C'est une *vieille* amie.**

a Cette voiture est (inférieur).
b Les bâtiments (extérieur) sont très (ancien).
c Les enfants ne sont pas très (heureux).
d Ce (vieux) monsieur est son père.
e Elle arrive avec un (vieux) ami.
f Il y a une (bref) pause dans le spectacle.
g Il y avait des accidents (*nmpl*) (fatal).
h Ce sont des enfants tout à fait (*completely*) (normal).
i Ce sont mes (nouveau) amies (français).

Exercise 13 (Unit 19)

Translate the following sentences into French.
a *My mother is Spanish.*
b *I have some fresh lemonade.*

c *It's an old hotel.*
d *It's a big room.*
e *He has a new red car.*
f *This is the last bottle.*
g *The first coach (**le car**) is in front of the white building.*
h *All the children are on the coach.*

Exercise 14 (Unit 20)

Write a sentence about each illustration using the words in the box.

E.g. Cette veste coûte 160 €.

| le T-shirt | la chemise | le pantalon | les chaussures |

Exercise 15 (Unit 23)

Insert the adverbs correctly in the following sentences.

E.g. La lettre est *enfin* arrivée.

a Elle est partie. *déjà*
b J'ai voulu y aller. *toujours*
c Il est arrivé. *tard*
d Vous avez travaillé. *bien*
e Elle a attendu. *patiemment*
f Ils sont arrivés. *hier*
g Tu as bu. *trop*
h Il est parti. *vite*
i C'est impossible. *absolument*
j Je suis en retard. *souvent*
k Elle va arriver. *après-demain*
l Je parlais. *franchement*
m Vous avez mangé. *beaucoup*
n Elle a fini. *vite*
o Vous avez tort. *rarement*
p Tu as conduit. *prudemment*
q Vous êtes parti. *très tôt*

Exercise 16 (Unit 24)

Look at the following sentence.

Georges est petit. (*more ... than*) → Il est plus petit que son frère.

Now follow the same process with the following sentences using *que son frère* at the end of each sentence.

a Colette est polie. (*more ... than*)
b Yves est patient. (*less ... than*)
c Michel est fort (*strong*). (*as ... as*)
d Anne-Marie est chic. (*less ... than*)
e Cécile est riche (*more ... than*)
f Hélène est active (*as ... as*)
g Simone est paresseuse (*lazy*) (*less ... than*)
h Julien n'est pas intelligent. (*as ... as*)

Exercise 17 (Unit 24)

Translate the following into French.

a *This hotel is better than the other.*
b *Jean-Pierre has more money than Daniel.*
c *Sylvie is younger than her sister.*
d *This coffee is stronger than the other.*
e *Jules is smaller than his brother.*
f *The beach is worse than the beach at Biarritz.*
g *This film is more interesting than the other.*

Exercise 18 (Unit 25)

Translate the following into French.

a *I go to the cinema more regularly now.*
b *He plays the piano as well as Charles.*
c *She speaks French faster now.*
d *He works more slowly than Jean.*

Exercise 19 (Unit 26)

Complete the sentences using superlatives forms. Remember that the adjectives must agree with the nouns.

E.g. Elle a acheté la bague (*ring*) la _____ (cher) → Elle a acheté la bague la plus chère.

a C'est le _____ festival de France. (grand)

b Ils ont la _____ maison de la ville. (beau)

c C'est la _____ montagne d'Europe. (haut)

d C'était l'expérience la _____ de ma vie. (mauvais)

e Elle est la _____ musicienne de tous. (bon)

f Cette ville est la _____ de la région. (important)

g C'est la raison la _____ . (stupide)

Exercise 20 (Unit 30)

Now underline the verbs in this French passage. One has been done for you.

Ma journée typique <u>commence</u> à six heures, quand je me lève. Je pars pour le bureau vers sept heures et demie. Je prends le train. Je mange à midi à la cantine. Je finis vers cinq heures. Le soir, on mange à sept heures et après je regarde la télévision ou je lis un peu. Quelquefois j'ai du travail à faire.

Exercise 21 (Unit 31)

By looking at the endings of the following verbs, and at the English sentences, fill in the correct subject pronoun (*je*, *tu*, etc.)

E.g. *Nous* préparons un repas. *We are preparing a meal.*

a _____ arrive à la gare. *He arrives at the station.*

b _____ aimons le vin. *We like wine.*

c _____ préparez les papiers. *You prepare the papers.*

d _____ travaille au centre de Paris. *I work in the centre of Paris.*

e _____ joues au tennis? *Do you play tennis?*

Exercise 22 (Unit 32)

Insert the correct subject to match the verb. (For some verbs there is more than one possible subject.)

E.g. _____ essayons. → Nous essayons.

a _____ commencez   f _____ répètes

b _____ jette   g _____ partagez

c _____ achètent   h _____ jetons

d _____ mangeons   i _____ avance

e _____ emploie   j _____ espère

Exercise 23 (Unit 33)

Match the words in the left-hand list with those on the right to make the English sentences below.

E.g. Je + finis vers six heures. *I finish at about six o'clock.*

a	J'	l	offrons un cadeau.
b	Elles	m	cueillent des fleurs.
c	Il	n	remplissez la fiche.
d	Nous	o	attends un bus.
e	Vous	p	ouvre la porte.
f	Tu	q	choisit une chemise rouge.
g	Ils	r	grossissent.
h	Elle	s	maigrissez, Michel!
i	Je	t	rougit.
j	Vous	u	réussis.
k	Je	v	finis vers six heures.

1 *They are picking flowers.*
2 *We give a gift.*
3 *I am succeeding.*
4 *You wait for a bus.*
5 *I open the door.*
6 *She is blushing.*
7 *He chooses a red shirt.*
8 *They are putting on weight.*
9 *You are losing weight, Michel!*
10 *You fill in the form.*
11 *I finish at about six o'clock.*

Exercise 24 (Unit 34)

Translate the following into French.

a *I'm selling this bike.*
b *They're waiting for the train.*
c *He's coming down the mountain now.*
d *She replies to the letter.*

Exercise 25 (Unit 35)

Fill in the missing words. The translation below may help you.

Je **me réveille** à sept heures. Je _____ dix minutes plus tard, puis je _____ dans la salle de bains. Je _____ . Puis je bois une tasse de café dans la cuisine. En général, je mange des toasts, puis je _____ les dents. Le weekend je _____ à neuf heures, et quelquefois je _____ en ville.

I wake up at seven o'clock. I get up ten minutes later, then I get washed in the bathroom. I get dressed. Then I drink a cup of coffee in the kitchen. Usually I eat some toast, then I brush my teeth. At the weekend I get up at nine o'clock, and sometimes I go for a walk in town.

Exercise 26 (Unit 36)

Give the correct subject pronoun as shown by the form of the verb and by the English.

E.g. _____ allons. *We go.* → Nous allons.

a _____ porte. *I carry.*

b _____ mangent. *They eat.* (feminine)

c _____ travaillons. *We work.*

d _____ part. *She leaves.*

e _____ finit. *He finishes.*

f _____ finis. *You finish.* (familiar)

g _____ arrive. *He arrives.*

h _____ partez. *You leave.* (plural)

i _____ vont. *They go.* (masculine)

j _____ changez. *You change.* (formal)

k _____ mange. *One eats.*

l _____ tombe. *It's falling.*

Exercise 27 (Unit 37)

Replace the *nous* form with *on* in the following sentences, choosing the verb from among those in the box.

E.g. Nous partons bientôt? *Shall we leave soon?* → On part bientôt?

| prend | lit | ~~part~~ | aime | fait | va | sort | choisit |

a Nous aimons bien le vin rouge. *We really like red wine.*
b Nous allons au cinéma plus tard. *We're going to the cinema later.*
c Nous prenons du poisson. *We'll have fish.*
d Nous faisons du vélo cet après-midi? *Shall we go for a cycle ride this afternoon?*

Exercise 28 (Unit 38)

Match the following sentences and then insert an appropriate emphatic pronoun.

E.g. Ce stylo est à _____ . *This pen is mine.* → Ce stylo est à *moi*.

a Ce journal est à _____ , l'autre est à _____ .
b J'ai écrit la lettre pour _____ .
c Ils partent sans _____ !
d Ce porte-clés n'est pas à _____ .

1 *I wrote the letter for them.*
2 *This newspaper is mine, the other is his.*
3 *This keyring is not ours.*
4 *They are leaving without us!*

Exercise 29 (Unit 39)

Choose suitable possessive pronouns from the box to complete the sentences, using the English as a guide.

E.g. Louis a une nouvelle bicyclette. Moi aussi – tu as vu *la mienne*? *Louis has a new bicycle. Me too – have you seen mine?*

les miennes	les miens	les nôtres	~~la mienne~~
au tien	les nôtres	les vôtres	des siens
aux miennes	les leurs	le leur	la tienne
	aux tiennes	à la tienne	

a Voici tes disquettes – où sont _____ ? *Here are your discs – where are mine?*

b Il a besoin de ses livres. A-t-elle besoin _____ ? *He needs his books. Does she need hers?*

c Ils ont leurs valises. Où sont _____? *They've got their suitcases. Where are yours?*

d Elle a son passeport. Où sont _____? *She's got her passport. Where are ours?*

e Je l'ai expliqué à mon frère. Tu l'as expliqué _____? *I have explained it to my brother. Have you explained it to yours?*

Exercise 30 (Unit 40)

Match the French with the English.

E.g. C'est à moi, ça! → *That's mine, that is!*

a Ceci est très amusant!

b Cela n'est pas vrai.

c Prenez ceci.

d Ce n'est pas facile.

e Écoutez cela!

1 *It isn't easy.*

2 *Take this.*

3 *This is very amusing!*

4 *Listen to that!*

5 *That's not true.*

Exercise 31 (Unit 41)

Complete the following sentences with *qui* or *que*.

E.g. Le musée _____ nous allons visiter s'appelle le musée Grévin. → Le musée *que* nous allons visiter s'appelle le musée Grévin. *The museum that we are going to visit is called the musée Grévin.*

a La personne _____ travaille dans ce bureau s'appelle Madame Gilles. *The person who works in this office is called Madame Gilles.*

b Le film _____ j'ai vu hier soir était très bon. *The film that I saw last night was very good.*

c Les croissants _____ tu as achetés sont excellents. *The croissants that you bought are excellent.*

d Je travaille au musée, _____ est en face de la bibliothèque. *I work at the museum, which is opposite the library.*

e Le restaurant _____ je préfère est à dix minutes d'ici. *The restaurant that I like best is ten minutes from here.*

f L'équipe _____ a gagné le match était très forte. *The team that won the match was really good.*

g Le jeune homme _____ joue du piano est mon cousin. *The young man who is playing the piano is my cousin.*

h Le dépliant _____ je cherchais était dans le tiroir. *The leaflet, which I was looking for, was in the drawer.*

i Le porte-monnaie _____ elle a trouvé est vide. *The purse that she found is empty.*

j Les bureaux _____ nous avons achetés se trouvent au rez-de-chaussée. *The offices that we have bought are on the ground floor.*

Exercise 32 (Unit 42)

Match the two parts of the sentences in French to correspond to the appropriate English sentences.

E.g. C'est la personne + dont tu parles. *It's the person you are talking about.*

a Ce sont les papiers

b C'est la maison

c C'est l'enfant

d C'est le jour

e C'est l'année

f où tu es allé en France.

g où nous sommes partis en vacances.

h dont je rêvais.

i dont il a besoin.

j dont il parle.

1 *It's the child he's talking about.*
2 *It's the day we went on holiday.*
3 *These are the papers he needs.*

4 *It's the house I dreamt of.*
5 *It's the year you went to France.*

Exercise 33 (Unit 43)

Complete the gaps in these sentences using *auquel*, *à laquelle*, *auxquels*, *auxquelles* or *à qui* as appropriate.

E.g. Je lui ai donné le numéro du bureau *auquel* il faut téléphone. *I have given him the number of the office that he must telephone.*

a Vous avez posé des questions _____ je ne peux pas répondre. *You have asked questions that I can't answer.*

b Est-ce que c'est l'homme _____ vous avez parlé? *Is it the man you spoke to?*

c C'est la date avant _____ je dois rentrer. *That's the date that I must return by.*

Exercise 34 (Unit 44)

Use *ce qui* or *ce que/ce qu'* to join the two halves of each sentence. The English translations are overleaf.

E.g. Il veut savoir + nous avons écrit. → *He wants to know what we have written.*

a Vous devez décider	g est suprenant.
b Elle avait oublié	h elle allait dire.
c Je ne sais pas	i tu as fait en vacances.
d Il est en retard	j va se passer.
e Dis-moi	k il a fait.
f Je voudrais savoir	l vous voulez faire.

1 *You must decide what you want to do.*
2 *She had forgotten what she was going to say.*
3 *I don't know what is going to happen.*
4 *He's late, which is surprising.*
5 *Tell me what you did on holiday.*
6 *I'd like to know what he's done.*

Exercise 35 (Unit 45)

**Complete the sentences by selecting an appropriate object
pronoun from the box, using the English sentences to guide you.**

E.g. Il veut _____ garder. *He wants to keep them.* → Il veut
les garder.

a Hélène rencontre **Yves** au cinéma.

| l' | le | les | leur |

Hélène _____ rencontre au cinéma.
Hélène meets him at the cinema.

b Jeanne dit au revoir **à ses amis.**

Jeanne _____ dit au revoir. *Jeanne says goodbye to them.*

c Il contrôle **les billets.**

Il _____ contrôle. *He checks them.*

Exercise 36 (Unit 46)

**The answers to the following questions below are incomplete.
Complete them by adding *y* or *en*.**

E.g. Il a des cousins? *Has he got any cousins?* Oui, il a
plusieurs. → Oui, il *en* a plusieurs. *Yes, he's got several.*

a Vous avez des livres sur la région? *Have you got any books on the area?* Oui, j'ai plusieurs. *Yes, I've got several.*

b Tu vas souvent au théâtre? *Do you often go to the theatre?* Oui, je vais deux fois par mois. *Yes, I go twice a month.*

c Vous avez combien d'amis à Tours? *How many friends have you got in Tours?* J'ai trois. *I've got three.*

d Vous habitez en France depuis longtemps? *Have you lived in France for long?* J'habite depuis trois ans. *I've lived there for three years.*

Exercise 37 (Unit 47)

Match the English and French sentences.

E.g. Les as-tu mangés? → *Have you eaten them?*

a Veux-tu l'acheter?	**1** *They sell them.*
b Le mangez-vous?	**2** *He telephones me every day.*
c Ils les vendent.	**3** *They sell it.*
d Donnez-le-lui.	**4** *Do you eat it?*
e Il me téléphone chaque jour.	**5** *Listen to him.*
f Veux-tu les acheter?	**6** *Do you want to buy it?*
g Écoutez-le.	**7** *Do you want to buy them?*
h Elles le vendent.	**8** *Give it to him.*

Exercise 38 (Unit 47)

Fill in the gaps in the following sentences by selecting appropriate object pronouns from the box.

E.g. Henri donne *le cadeau* à son ami. → Henri *le lui* donne. *Henri gives it to him.*

la	le	les	lui	leur

a Jean-Luc raconte **l'histoire à son fils.**
   Jean-Luc _____ raconte. *Jean-Luc tells it to him.*
b Elle donne **les journaux à son patron.**
   Elle _____ donne. *She gives them to him.*
c Marc demande **les documents à ses collègues.**
   Marc _____ demande. *He asks them for them.*
d Alice donne **le thé à son amie.**
   Alice _____ donne. *She gives it to her.*

Exercise 39 (Unit 50)

Using *aller* and an infinitive, complete the list of the right to say what is going to happen tomorrow.

E.g. Aujourd'hui, je regarde la télévision. Demain, je vais regarder la télévision.

AUJOURD'HUI	DEMAIN
a Elle range son bureau.	_____
b Ils jouent aux boules.	_____

c Tu prends un café. _____

d Nous écoutons la radio. _____

e Il mange à la cantine. _____

f J'écris une lettre au client. _____

g Elles choisissent un cadeau. _____

h Il achète un ordinateur. _____

i Il fait beau. _____

Exercise 40 (Unit 50)

Using *aller* or *faire* say what the following people are doing.

E.g. Elles font du vélo.

a

b

c

Exercise 41 (Unit 52)

Make sentences from the columns to match the English ones.

E.g. Je veux + aller + en France. *I want to go to France.*

Est-ce que tu peux	aller	la fenêtre?
Je voudrais	fermer	ce soir?
Veux-tu	sortir	une tasse de thé?
Je peux	prendre	une veste.
Je veux	acheter	la porte?
Vous voulez	ouvrir	en France.
Pouvez-vous	faire	du ski.
Elle veut		

a *Would you like to have a cup of tea?*
b *Can you open the door?*
c *Do you want to go out this evening?*
d *I want to buy a jacket.*
e *She wants to go to France.*
f *Can I shut the window?*
g *I would like to go skiing.*

Exercise 42 (Unit 53)

Make sentences that correspond to the English sentences given below.

E.g. Elle doit + faire + la cuisine. *She must do the cooking.*

Dois-je	aller	avant dix heures?
Elle sait	faire	la cuisine.
Elle doit	rentrer	à Rouen.
Savez-vous	finir	bientôt.
Nous devons		de la voile.
Sait-il		du ski?
Doivent-ils		

a *Do I have to come home before ten o'clock?*

b *She knows how to cook.*

c *We have to finish soon.*

d *Do you know how to ski?*

c *She has to go to Rouen.*

f *Does he know how to sail?*

Exercise 43 (Unit 55)

Write a sentence using the language in the box to show what the following people are doing.

> écouter   faire le repassage   se doucher   manger   chanter
> regarder la télé

a

b

c

Exercise 44 (Unit 58)

Make sentences from the following using the English sentences as a guide.

E.g. Il est facile + d' + oublier un visage. *It's easy to forget a face.*

Elles continuent	à	lire le journal.
Il oublie toujours		acheter du lait.
Il commence		partir en vacances.
Ils essayent	de (d')	bavarder.
Nous allons essayer		rester à la maison.
Elle hésite		nous accompagner.
Ils sont contents		revenir bientôt.

a *They continue to chat.*
b *He always forgets to buy milk.*
c *He is starting to read the paper.*
d *They are trying to come with us.*
e *We'll try to come back soon.*
f *She's hesitating about going on holiday.*
g *They are happy to stay at home.*

Exercise 45 (Unit 59)

Make sentences from the following using the English as a guide.

E.g. J' + aide + nos amis à laver la voiture. *I am helping our friends to wash the car.*

Philippe	aident	nos amis à déjeuner avec nous.
Nous	oblige	mon fils à faire ses devoirs.
J'	aide	leur père à laver la voiture.
Marie	encourage	son frère à prendre une décision.
Ils	allons inviter	son ami à écrire la lettre.

a *Philippe helps his friend to write the letter.*
b *We are going to invite our friends to have lunch with us.*
c *I encourage my son to do his homework.*
d *Marie is forcing her brother to make a decision.*
e *They help their father to wash the car.*

Exercise 46 (Unit 63)

Insert the appropriate past participle from amongst those in the box into the gaps in the following sentences.

E.g. Regarde mes chaussures. Je les ai _____ ce matin. →
    Regarde mes chaussures. Je les ai *achetées* ce matin.

| vu | choisie | achetée | choisi | laissés | laissé | achetés |
| mis | faite | visités | vue | achetées | mises | fait | visité |

a Tu as perdu tes crayons? Non, je les ai _____ chez moi.

b Ces fleurs? Je les ai _____ au marché.

c Le film français? Je l'ai _____ hier soir.

d Les chaussettes? Il les a _____ dans la valise.

e Voilà le musée que nous avons _____ la semaine dernière.

f Voici la voiture que j'ai _____ hier.

g C'est le gâteau qu'il a _____ .

Exercise 47 (Unit 64)

Correct the information under each of the following pictures.

E.g. Elle faisait la cuisine. → Non. Elle écrivait une lettre.

Il jouait au golf.   Elles travaillaient à l'ordinateur.   Elle lisait un livre.

Exercise 48 (Unit 65)

Rewrite the following passage using the perfect and imperfect tenses instead of the present.

C'est le 22 août, et il fait très chaud. Je me promène quand je rencontre mon amie Catherine. Nous décidons de prendre un café ensemble. Pendant que nous buvons un café, nous voyons un petit accident au coin de la rue. Deux voitures se heurtent l'une contre l'autre et les deux hommes qui conduisent commencent à se disputer.

Exercise 49 (Unit 66)

Now complete the following sentences with the pluperfect tense of the verb given in brackets.

E.g. Vous _____ _____ et on n'a pas pu vous trouver.
(partir) → Vous *étiez partis* et on n'a pas pu vous trouver.

a J'_____ déjà _____ le dessert quand ils sont arrivés.
(préparer)

b Elle _____ _____ à l'heure et voulait prendre le train.
(arriver)

c Il _____ _____ son portefeuille en route pour l'aéroport.
(perdre)

d Nous nous _____ _____ de bonne heure pour voir le lever du soleil. (se réveiller)

e Elles _____ _____ leurs cartes postales et sont allées à la poste. (écrire)

f Avant de partir j'_____ _____ ma voiture. (laver)

g Je ne savais pas que tu _____ _____. (arriver)

Exercise 50 (Unit 67)

Rewrite the following paragraph, putting the verbs given in brackets into the past historic tense.

Minuit (sonner) (*struck*). Jean-Luc (entendre) quelque chose. Il (regarder) par la fenêtre et (voir) quelqu'un. Après un moment, on (frapper) à la porte. C'etait Gaston. « Vite, entre », (dire) Jean-Luc. Gaston (prendre) un morceau de papier dans sa poche, puis (lire) le message. Jean-Luc (écouter) attentivement. Ils (se regarder).

Exercise 51 (Unit 68)

Complete the following horoscopes, putting the appropriate verb in the box into the future tense and using each verb only once. The first one has been done for you.

acheter	recevoir (recevr-)	s'amuser	écrire	~~être~~

CAPRICORNE: Vous **serez** en forme, et vous _____ bien cette semaine. Vous _____ un cadeau, et le 30 _____ une journée exceptionnelle. Vous _____ beaucoup de lettres, et vous _____ quelque chose d'important.

| oublier | se disputer | aider | sortir | dépenser | avoir |

SCORPION: Vous _____ une semaine difficile. Vous _____ beaucoup et vous _____ trop d'argent. Vous _____ avec une amie et vous _____ une date importante. Mais d'autres amis vous _____ .

Exercise 52 (Unit 70)

Match the following questions and answers.

E.g. Qu'est-ce qu'il ferait s'il pleuvait? Il mettrait un anorak.

a Qu'est-ce qu'il ferait s'il avait faim?

b Qu'est-ce que vous feriez si vous étiez riche?

c Qu'est-ce qu'il ferait s'il était fatigué?

d Qu'est-ce que vous feriez si vous aviez soif?

e Qu'est-ce qu'ils feraient s'ils gagnaient à la Loterie nationale?

f Qu'est-ce que vous feriez si vous aviez plus de temps libre?

g Qu'est-ce qu'elles feraient, si elles étaient libres ce soir?

1 Je boirais quelque chose.

2 Ils feraient le tour de monde.

3 Elles iraient au théâtre.

4 Il mangerait un grand repas.

5 Nous lirions et nous regarderions la télé!

6 J'achèterais une maison en France.

7 Il dormirait.

Exercise 53 (Unit 71)

Put the following into the conditional perfect, using the verb given in brackets and the English sentences as a guide.

E.g. Si Jean-Paul était arrivé, nous _____ manger ensemble. (pouvoir) *If Jean-Paul had arrived we could have eaten together.* → Si Jean-Paul était arrivé, nous aurions pu manger ensemble.

a S'il avait eu l'argent, René _____ _____ le TGV. (prendre)
  If he had had the money René would have taken the TGV.

b Si elle s'était levée, elle _____ _____ à l'heure. (partir)
  If she had got up, she would have left on time.

c Si les documents étaient arrivés, André _____ _____ son travail. (commencer)
  If the documents had arrived, André would have started his work.

d Si elle avait su que c'était son anniversaire, Aimée _____ _____ un gâteau. (faire)
  If she had known that it was his/her birthday, Aimée would have made a cake.

e S'il avait plu, Michel et Françoise _____ _____ chez eux. (rester)
  If it had rained Michel and Françoise would have stayed at home.

Exercise 54 (Unit 74)

Fill the gaps using the tense indicated and the verb in brackets.

E.g. (*present*) *Je suis invité(e)* à la réunion. (inviter) *I am invited to the reunion.*

Present

a Ils _____ par tout le monde. (aimer) *They are liked by everyone.*

b Le jardin _____ par mon ami. (soigner) *The garden is tended by my friend.*

Perfect

c Le vase _____ . (casser) *The vase has been broken.*

d Tous les sandwichs _____ . (manger) *All the sandwiches have been eaten.*

Imperfect

e Le pont _____ souvent. (repeindre) *The bridge was often repainted.*

f Les malades _____ par deux infirmières. (soigner) *The patients were looked after by two nurses.*

Pluperfect

g Les boissons _____ . (servir) *Drinks had been served.*

h La voiture _____ . (vendre) *The car had been sold.*

Future

i Il _____ par le policier. (interroger) *He will be questioned by the policeman.*

j Le paquet _____ demain. (livrer) *The parcel will be delivered tomorrow.*

Conditional

k Le musée _____ par la municipalité. (fermer) *The museum would be closed by the council.*

l Le déjeuner _____ à midi. (servir) *Lunch would be served at midday.*

Exercise 55 (Unit 75)

Complete the following sentences by putting the verbs in brackets into the *je* form of the present subjunctive. Each sentence begins with *Il faut que je* (*It is necessary that I/I must*)

E.g. _____ (écrire) des lettres. → Il faut que j'écrive des lettres. Il faut que je...

a _____ (apprendre) mes verbes. *learn my verbs*

b _____ (aller) en France. *go to France*

c _____ (choisir) une nouvelle voiture. *choose a new car*

d _____ (lire) ce livre. *read this book*

e _____ (être) patient. *be patient*

f _____ (venir) te voir. *come and see you*

g _____ (prendre) des notes. *take notes*

Exercise 56 (Unit 77)

Form the following sentences from the two columns below using the English sentences to guide you.

E.g. Je doute + qu'elle ait terminé le programme. *I doubt whether she's finished the programme.*

a Je suis content
b Elle est furieuse
c Je suis très fière
d Je suis triste
e Je ne crois pas
f Il craint
g Il nie

h que vous partiez.
i qu'elle n'attende pas.
j que tu reçoives le prix.
k qu'il ne soit pas à l'heure.
l que vous puissiez venir.
m que tu sois malade.
n qu'ils viennent me voir.

1 *He is afraid that she will not wait.*
2 *She is furious that he is not on time.*
3 *I'm pleased that you can come.*
4 *I'm very proud that you are receiving the prize.*
5 *I'm sad that you are leaving.*
6 *I don't believe that you are ill.*
7 *He denies that they're coming to see me.*

Exercise 57 (Unit 79)

Select the correct option to complete the following sentences.

E.g. Je voudrais parler à quelqu'un qui sait/*sache* son numéro de téléphone. *I'd like to talk to someone who knows his telephone number.*

a Il cherche quelqu'un qui sait/sache la verité. *He is looking for someone who knows the truth.*

b Vous cherchez un médecin qui peut/puisse l'aider? *Are you looking for a doctor who can help her?*

c J'ai trouvé un électricien qui peut/puisse venir. *I've found an electrician who can come.*

d C'est la seule chose qu'il sait/sache faire. *It's the only thing he knows how to do.*

e C'est le meilleur film que j'ai/aie jamais vu. *It's the best film I've ever seen.*

Exercise 58 (Unit 82)

Match the following sentence halves to make full sentences.

E.g. **Pauline n'est + jamais chez elle.**

a Sophie ne range	**1**	personne dans sa voiture.
b Il n'aime	**2**	jamais gentille.
c Vous ne sortez	**3**	que des légumes. Elle est végétarienne.
d Il n'y a	**4**	pas le vin rouge. Il préfère le vin blanc.
e Jean-Paul ne prend	**5**	rien à voir ici.
f Elle ne mange	**6**	jamais sa chambre.
g Jeanne n'est	**7**	pas le weekend.

Exercise 59 (Unit 83)

Make the following sentences negative by using *ne ... pas*.

E.g. Je suis allée en ville ce matin. → Je ne suis pas allée en ville ce matin.

a Il a compris le problème.

b Elle s'est levée de bonne heure.

c Il aurait fini le projet.

d Elle avait écrit une lettre.

e J'aurais acheté la robe bleue.

f Nous sommes arrivés à l'heure.

Exercise 60 (Unit 83)

Make the following sentences negative, using the form in brackets.

E.g. Les a-t-il vus? (ne ... pas) → Ne les a-t-il pas vus?

a Y vas-tu? (ne ... pas)

b Me les as-tu donnés? (ne ... pas)

c A-t-il vendu quatre voitures? (ne ... que)

d Avez-vous vu? (ne ... personne)

e A-t-elle laissé un mot? (ne ... aucun)

Exercise 61 (Unit 84)

What was the question that prompted each of these answers? For each answer give two question forms, as in the example.

E.g. Oui, je suis marié. → Vous êtes marié? Êtes-vous marié?

a Oui, j'ai une voiture.

b Oui, je vais au cinéma ce soir.

c Non, je ne veux pas sortir.

d Non, je ne suis pas agriculteur, je suis pêcheur.

e Non, nous parlons français.

f Oui, je voudrais bien prendre un congé.

Exercise 62 (Unit 86)

Match the parts of the sentences, using the English below as a guide.

E.g. Lequel + des dictionnaires veux-tu? *Which of the dictionaries do you want?*

a Lequel		i	veux-tu prendre?
b Qui		j	de ces robes veux-tu acheter?
c Il y a deux voitures. Laquelle		k	veut-il accompagner?
d Qui		l	vous a donné cela?
e De quoi		m	est-ce que tu es venu?
f Pour qui		n	des théâtres préférez-vous?
g Laquelle		o	travailles-tu?
h Avec qui		p	parlez-vous?

1 *Which of the theatres do you prefer?*

2 *Who gave you that?*

3 *Who does he want to go with?*

4 *There are two cars. Which one do want to take?*

5 *Which of these dresses do you want to buy?*

6 *What are you talking about?*

7 *Who do you work for?*

8 *Who did you come with?*

Exercise 63 (Unit 87)

Insert the missing numbers in the following sequences.

E.g. un, deux, **trois**, quatre, cinq, **six**, sept

a deux, quatre, six, _____ , dix, douze, quatorze, _____

b un, trois, _____ , sept, neuf, _____ , treize

c dix-huit, _____ , douze, neuf, _____ , trois

d cinq, _____ , quinze, _____ , vingt-cinq

Exercise 64 (Unit 88)

Follow the example to say where the following people live. Use the initials in the diagram to work out who's who.

E.g. Jean habite au _____ étage (*floor/storey*). → Jean habite au troisième étage.

Mr M Gabin (rez-de-chaussée)	
Mr et Mme P Boulanger (1er étage)	
Mlles C et P Durand (2e étage)	
Mr J Dupont (3e étage)	
Mlle S Duplessis (4e étage)	
Mr H Mangin (5e étage)	
Mme J Etienne (6e étage)	

a Cathérine et Pascale habitent au _____ étage.

b Pierre et Sophie habitent au _____ étage.

c Stéphanie habite au _____ étage.

d Henri habite au _____ étage.
e Jeanne habite au _____ étage.
f Jacques habite au _____ étage.

Exercise 65 (Unit 89)

Complete the following sentences using the information in the graph.

E.g. Cinq pour cent (*per cent*) vont en Allemagne.

De ceux qui ont répondu au questionnaire sur les vacances –

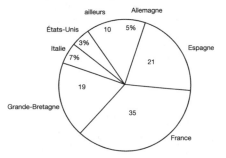

a _____ vont en Espagne.
b _____ vont en France.
c _____ vont en Grande-Bretagne.
d _____ vont en Italie.
e _____ vont aux États-Unis.
f _____ vont ailleurs (*elsewhere*).

Exercise 66 (Unit 90)

Translate the following sentences into French.

E.g. I live 10 kilometres from here. → **J'habite à 10 kilomètres d'ici.**

a *Toulouse is 80 kilometres from here.*

b *We're half an hour away from home* (**de chez nous**).

c *How far is the nearest garage?*

d *It must be at least* (**au moins**) *20 kilometres from here.*

e *The bank is only 5 minutes away.*

Exercise 67 (Unit 91)

Complete the sentences with the appropriate time.

E.g. **Barbara se lève à** _____ . **Barbara se lève à** *sept heures.*

a À _____ elle prend son petit déjeuner. (7h20)

b À _____ elle quitte la maison. (8h10)

c Elle commence son travail à _____. (8h55)

d À _____ elle déjeune. (12h45)

e À_____ elle fait les courses. (18h00)

Exercise 68 (Unit 91)

State the following times in full using the 24-hour clock.

E.g. 13h22 → treize heures vingt-deux.

a 17h40   c 19h25   e 15h15

b 03h35   d 12h22   f 18h30

Exercise 69 (Unit 92)

Look at the following calendar and write down the dates circled.

E.g. dimanche, le trois janvier *Sunday, 3 January*

Janvier

L		4	11	18	25
M		5	12	19	26
M		6	13	20	27
J		7	14	21	28
V	1	8	15	22	29
S	2	9	16	23	30
D	3	10	17	24	31

Février

L	1	8	15	22
M	2	9	16	23
M	3	10	17	24
J	4	11	18	25
V	5	12	19	26
S	6	13	20	27
D	7	14	21	28

Mars

L	1	8	15	22	29
M	2	9	16	23	30
M	3	10	17	24	31
J	4	11	18	25	
V	5	12	19	26	
S	6	13	20	27	
D	7	14	21	28	

Exercise 70 (Unit 93)

Match the sentences on the left with their meanings on the right.

E.g. Je suis étudiant ici depuis trois mois. *I've been a student here for three months.*

a Depuis quand lis-tu?

b Je l'ai vu il y a deux jours.

c Elle attendait depuis quinze minutes.

d Ils habitent à Chartres depuis deux mois.

e Ça faisait deux heures qu'il lisait.

f Elles habitaient à Chartres depuis deux mois.

g Je connais Pierre depuis dix ans.

h Il y a une heure qu'il parle.

i Je joue du violon depuis deux ans.

j Voilà un mois qu'elle habite ici.

1 *She had been waiting for fifteen minutes.*

2 *They have been living in Chartres for two months.*

3 *I saw him two days ago.*

4 *I have been playing the violin for two years.*

5 *He has been talking for an hour.*

6 *He had been reading for two hours.*

7 *How long have you been reading for?*

8 *I have known Pierre for ten years.*

9 *She's been living here for a month.*

10 *They had been living in Chartres for two months.*

Exercise 71 (Unit 93)

Insert *depuis* or *il y a* into the following sentences.

E.g. J'ai appris à nager _____ deux ans. → J'ai appris à nager *il y a* deux ans.

a Il est venu vous voir _____ vingt minutes.
b Je suis en vacances _____ deux jours.
c Je travaille comme institutrice _____ trois ans.
d Elle a vu le film _____ deux semaines.
e Nous sommes rentrés de Grenoble _____ un mois.
f Elles apprennent le chinois _____ un an.

Exercise 72 (Unit 94)

Translate the following sentences using the tense indicated.

E.g. *There are three cars in front of the house.* (present tense) → Il y a trois voitures devant la maison.

a *There will be fireworks in front of the town hall* (**la mairie**). (future tense)
b *There were bottles in the fridge.* (imperfect tense)
c *There are vegetables in the soup* (**la soupe**). (present tense)
d *There has been a mistake* (**une erreur**). (perfect tense)
e *There will be a lot of people* (**beaucoup de monde**) *at the cinema.* (future tense)
f *There were children in the park.* (imperfect tense)
g *There is some money in my pocket* (**la poche**). (present tense)

Exercise 73 (Unit 96)

Complete the table. One has been done for you.

Country/Continent	Masculine adjective	Feminine adjective
a la France	français	**française**
b		italienne
c	japonais	
d le Canada		
e l'Angleterre	anglais	
f les États-Unis	américain	
g		espagnole
h	luxembourgeois	
i la Chine		chinoise
j l'Afrique	africain	

Exercise 74 (Unit 99)

Complete the following sentences and match them to their English equivalents.

a Il y a
b Ils ont acheté
c J'ai quelques
d On m'a offert
e J'ai besoin d'acheter
f Tu voudrais
g Il y a plusieurs
h Il a moins de responsabilités

i euros à dépenser.
j quelques légumes.
k tant de cadeaux.
l journaux à lire.
m plusieurs possibilités.
n que moi.
o un verre de vin rouge?
p six tranches de jambon.

1 *They have bought six slices of ham.*
2 *I have a few euros to spend.*
3 *I need to buy a few vegetables.*
4 *He has fewer responsibilities than I.*
5 *I've been given so many presents.*
6 *Would you like a glass of red wine?*
7 *There are several newspapers to read.*
8 *There are several possibilities.*

Exercise 1 (Unit 1):

l e v i n	o s t f m
p t	l m y r l n y p
s	l e l a i t	q r b
l	a c h e m i s e	t
i r h f	l e p l a n
m a i	l a c r e m e
a d e e	l h o m m e
g i n p v x a n l n	
e	o c r p	l a r u e
o	l a v o i t u r e

Exercise 2 (Unit 1): a les journaux **b** les banques **c** les voix **d** les fromages **e** les bateaux **f** les cinémas

Exercise 3 (Unit 2): a un; des **b** une; des **c** des; de; des; des

Exercise 4 (Unit 5): a un pied **b** un bras **c** un nez **d** un cheval **e** un livre **f** des téléviseurs **g** des lampes **h** un cinéma **i** une église **j** une docteur

Exercise 5 (Unit 7): a le beau-père **b** le haut-parleur **c** le porte-clefs **d** le chef-d'oeuvre **e** le rouge-gorge **f** l'oiseau-mouche

Exercise 6 (Unit 8): 1 e 2 a 3 f 4 c 5 d 6 b

Exercise 7 (Unit 11): a entre **b** malgré **c** en **d** en; en **e** en; en

Exercise 8 (Unit 13): a Voici la valise d'Hélène. **b** C'est l'appartement de Jean. **c** Le train arrive à six heures du soir. **d** J'aime la couleur des bicyclettes/vélos.

Exercise 9 (Unit 14): Your sentences should include the following links: à la pâtisserie; à l'école; au cinéma; à la pharmacie; aux magasins; à l'église; au café; à Montpellier

Exercise 10 (Unit 16): a sa; ses; ses; son **b** sa; ses **c** votre **d** tes **e** sa **f** leurs **g** notre **h** ses

Exercise 11 (Unit 17): a blanches; petite **b** bon; chère; grande **c** espagnole; jolie; long; noirs; bruns

Exercise 12 (Unit 18): a inférieure **b** extérieurs; anciens **c** heureux **d** vieux **e** vieil **f** brève **g** fatals **h** normaux **i** nouvelles; françaises

Exercise 13 (Unit 19): a Ma mère est espagnole. **b** J'ai de la limonade fraîche. **c** C'est un vieil hôtel. **d** C'est une grande pièce. **e** Il a une nouvelle voiture rouge. **f** C'est la dernière bouteille. **g** Le premier car est devant le bâtiment blanc. **h** Tous les enfants sont dans le car.

Exercise 14 (Unit 20): a Ce pantalon coûte 65 €. **b** Ce tee-shirt coûte 16 €. **c** Ces chaussures coûtent 80 €. **d** Cette chemise coûte 40 €.

Exercise 15 (Unit 23): a Elle est déjà partie. **b** J'ai toujours voulu y aller. **c** Il est arrivé tard. **d** Vous avez bien travaillé.   e Elle a attendu patiemment.   f Ils sont arrivés hier.   g Tu as trop bu.   h Il est vite parti.   i C'est absolument impossible.   j Je suis souvent en retard. k Elle va arriver après demain.   l Je parlais franchement. m Vous avez beaucoup mangé.   n Elle a vite fini.   o Vous avez rarement tort.   p Tu as conduis prudemment.   q Vous êtes parti très tôt.

Exercise 16 (Unit 24): a plus polie que son frère   **b** moins patient que …   **c** aussi fort que …   **d** moins chic que … **e** plus riche que …   **f** aussi active que …   **g** moins paresseuse que …   **h** n'est pas si intelligent que …

Exercise 17 (Unit 24): a Cet hôtel est meilleur que l'autre. **b** J-P a plus d'argent que D.   **c** S est plus jeune que sa sœur.   **d** Ce café est plus fort que l'autre.   **e** Jules est plus petit que son frère.   **f** La plage est moins bon / pire / plus mauvais que la plage à B.   **g** Ce film est plus intéressant que l'autre.

Exercise 18 (Unit 25): a Je vais au cinéma plus régulièrement maintenant.   **b** Il joue du piano aussi bien que Charles.   **c** Elle parle français plus vite maintenant. **d** Il travaille plus lentement que Jean.

Exercise 19 (Unit 26): a le plus grand festival   **b** la plus belle maison   **c** la plus haute montagne   **d** la plus mauvaise / la pire   **e** la meilleure musicienne   **f** la plus importante   **g** plus stupide

Exercise 20 (Unit 30): *The verbs are*: commence; (me) lève; pars; prends; mange; finis; mange; regarde; lis; ai; faire

Exercise 21 (Unit 31): a il b nous c vous d je e tu

Exercise 22 (Unit 32): a vous b je/il/elle c ils/elles d nous e j'/il\elle f tu g vous h nous i j'/il\elle j j'/il/elle

Exercise 23 (Unit 33): a p5 b r8 c q7 d l2 e s9 f o4 g m1 h t6 i u3 j n10

Exercise 24 (Unit 34): a Je vends ce vélo. b Ils attendent le train. c Il descend la montagne maintenant. d Elle répond à la lettre.

Exercise 25 (Unit 35): Je me lève; je me lave; Je m'habille; je me brosse les dents; je me lève; je me promène.

Exercise 26 (Unit 36): a je b Elles c Nous d Elle e Il f Tu g Il h Vous i Ils j Vous k On l Il/elle

Exercise 27 (Unit 37): a on aime b on va c on prend d on fait

Exercise 28 (Unit 38): a moi; lui 2 b eux; 1 c nous; 4 d nous; 3

Exercise 29 (Unit 39): a les miennes b des siens c les vôtres d les nôtres e au tien

Exercise 30 (Unit 40): a 3 b 5 c 2 d 1 e 4

Exercise 31 (Unit 41): a qui **b** que **c** que **d** qui
e que **f** qui **g** qui **h** que **i** qu' **j** que

Exercise 32 (Unit 42): a i3 **b** h4 **c** j1 **d** g2 **e** f5

Exercise 33 (Unit 43): a auxquelles **b** auquel/à qui
c laquelle

Exercise 34 (Unit 44): a ce que; l **b** ce qu'; h **c** ce qui; j
d de qui; g **e** ce que; i **f** ce qu'; k

Exercise 35 (Unit 45): a le **b** leur **c** les

Exercise 36 (Unit 46): a J'en ai plusieurs. **b** J'y vais deux
fois par mois. **c** J'en ai trois. **d** J'y habite depuis trois ans.

Exercise 37 (Unit 47): a 6 **b** 4 **c** 1 **d** 8 **e** 2 **f** 7
g 5 **h** 3

Exercise 38 (Unit 47): a la lui **b** les lui **c** les leue **d** le
lui

Exercise 39 (Unit 50): a Elle va ranger **b** Ils vont jouer
c Tu vas prendre **d** Nous allons écouter **e** Il va manger
f Je vais écrire **g** Elles vont choisir **h** Il va acheter **i** Il
va faire

Exercise 40 (Unit 50): a Ils vont à la piscine/vont faire de
la natation. **b** Elle fait du ski **c** Ils font de la voile.

Exercise 41 (Unit 52): a Vous voulez prendre une tasse de
thé? **b** Pouvez-vous/Est-ce que tu peux ouvrir la porte?

c Veux-tu/Voulez-vous/Tu veux/Vous voulez sortir ce soir?
d Je veux acheter une veste. **e** Elle veut aller en France.
f Puis-je fermer la fenêtre? **g** Je voudrais faire du ski.

Exercise 42 (Unit 53): a Dois-je rentrer avant 10 heures?
b Elle sait faire la cuisine **c** Nous devons finir bientôt.
d Savez-vous faire du ski? **e** Elle doit aller à Rouen.
f Sait-il faire de la voile?

Exercise 43 (Unit 55): a Elle écoute la radio en se douchant.
b Il chante en faisant le repassage. **c** Elle mange des chocolats/
bonbons en regardant la télévision.

Exercise 44 (Unit 58): a Elles continuent à bavarder. **b** Il
oublie toujours d'acheter du lait. **c** Il commence à lire le
journal. **d** Ils essayent de venir avec nous. **e** Nous allons
essayer de revenir bientôt. **f** Elle hésite de partir en
vacances. **g** Ils sont contents de rester à la maison.

Exercise 45 (Unit 59): a Philippe aide son ami à écrire la
lettre. **b** Nous allons inviter nos amis à déjeuner avec nous.
c J'encourage mon fils à faire ses devoirs. **d** Marie oblige
son frère à faire une décision. **e** Ils aident leur père à laver
la voiture

Exercise 46 (Unit 63): a laissés **b** achetées **c** vu
d mises **e** visité **f** achetée **g** choisi

Exercise 47 (Unit 64): a Il nageait **b** Elles regardaient la
télévision. **c** Elle faisait du ski.

Exercise 48 (Unit 65): C'était le … il faisait … Je me promenais … j'ai rencontré … Nous avons décidé … nous buvions … nous avons vu … se sont heurtées … conduisaient … ont commencé

Exercise 49 (Unit 66): a J'avais déjà préparé **b** était arrivée **c** avait perdu **d** étions réveillé(e)s **e** avaient écrit **f** j'avais lavé **g** étais arrivé(e)

Exercise 50 (Unit 67): sonna; entendit; regarda; vit; frappa; dit; prit; lut: écouta; se regardèrent

Exercise 51 (Unit 68): CAPRICORNE: vous vous amuserez; vous recevrez; le 30 sera; vous écrirez; vous achèterez; SCORPION: vous aurez; vous sortirez; dépenserez; vous vous disputerez; vous oublierez; (ils)…/aideront

Exercise 52 (Unit 70): a 4 **b** 6 **c** 7 **d** 1 **e** 2 **f** 5 **g** 3

Exercise 53 (Unit 71): a aurait pris **b** serait partie **c** aurait commencé **d** aurait fait **e** seraient restés

Exercise 54 (Unit 74): a sont aimés **b** est soigné **c** a été cassé **d** ont été mangés **e** était repeint **f** étaient soignés **g** avaient été servies **h** avait été vendue **i** sera interrogé **j** sera livré **k** serait fermé **l** serait servi

Exercise 55 (Unit 75): a j'apprenne **b** j'aille **c** je choisisse **d** je lise **e** je sois **f** je vienne **g** je prenne

Exercise 56 (Unit 77): a l3 **b** k2 **c** j4 **d** h5 **e** m6 **f** i1 **g** n7

Exercise 57 (Unit 79): a sache **b** puisse **c** peut
d sache **e** aie

Exercise 58 (Unit 82): a 6 **b** 4 **c** 7 **d** 5 **e** 1 **f** 3 **g** 2

Exercise 59 (Unit 83): a Il n'a pas compris le problème. **b**
Elle ne s'est pas levée … **c** Il n'aurait pas fini … **d** Elle
n'avait pas écrit … **e** Je n'aurais pas acheté. **f** Nous ne
sommes pas arrivés …

Exercise 60 (Unit 83): a N'y vas-tu pas? **b** Ne me les as-
tu pas donnés? **c** N'a-t-il vendu que quatre voitures?
d N'avez-vous vu personne? **e** N'a-t-elle laissé aucun mot?

Exercise 61 (Unit 84): (*The following feedback gives all
three possible answers in each case. The most likely form of
the second-person ('you') is used for each scenario, or both
where either is plausible.*) **a** Vous avez une voiture? Tu as
une voiture? Est-ce que vous avez une voiture? Est-ce que tu
as une voiture? Avez-vous une voiture? As-tu une voiture?
b Tu vas au cinéma ce soir? Est-ce que tu vas au cinéma ce
soir? Vas-tu au cinéma ce soir? **c** Tu veux sortir? Est-ce
que tu veux sortir? Veux-tu sortir? **d** Vous êtes agriculteur?
Est-ce que vous êtes agriculteur? Êtes-vous agriculteur?
e Vous parlez (anglais)? Est-ce que vous parlez (anglais)?
Parlez-vous (anglais)? **f** Tu voudrais prendre du congé?
Est-ce que tu voudrais prendre du congé? (*inversion is not
likely for this question*)

Exercise 62 (Unit 86): an1 bl2 ci4 dk3 ep6 fo7
gj5 hm8

Exercise 63 (Unit 87): a huit, seize (*two-times table*)
b cinq, onze (*odd numbers*) **c** quinze, six (*subtract*)
d dix, vingt (*five-times table*)

Exercise 64 (Unit 88): a deuxième **b** premier **c** quatrième
d cinquième **e** sixième **f** troisième

Exercise 65 (Unit 89): a Vingt-et-un pour cent …
b Trente-cinq pour cent … **c** Dix-neuf pour cent …
d Sept pour cent … **e** Trois pour cent … **f** Dix pour
cent …

Exercise 66 (Unit 90): a Toulouse est à 80 kilomètres d'ici.
b Nous sommes à une demi-heure de chez nous. **c** Le
garage le plus près est à combien d'ici? **d** Il doit être à au
moins 20 kilomètres d'ici. **e** La banque est à 5 minutes
(d'ici) seulement.

Exercise 67 (Unit 91): a sept heures vingt **b** huit heures
dix **c** neuf heures moins cinq **d** une heure moins le quart
e dix-huit heures

Exercise 68 (Unit 91): a dix-sept heures quarante **b** trois
heures trente-cinq **c** dix-neuf heures vingt-cinq **d** douze
heures vingt-deux **e** quinze heures quinze **f** dix-huit
heures trente

Exercise 69 (Unit 92): a vendredi, le 22 janvier b mardi, le 9 février c samedi, le 13 février d lundi, le 15 mars e mercredi, le 17 mars

Exercise 70 (Unit 93): a 7 b 3 c 1 d 2 e 6 f 10 g 8 h 5 i 4 j 9

Exercise 71 (Unit 93): a il y a b depuis c depuis d il y a e il y a f depuis

Exercise 72 (Unit 94): a Il y aura des feux d'artifice devant la mairie. b Il y avait des bouteilles dans le frigo. c Il y a des légumes dans la soupe. d Il y a eu une erreur. e Il y aura beaucoup de monde au cinéma. f Il y avait des enfants dans le parc. g Il y a de l'argent dans ma poche.

Exercise 73 (Unit 96): a française b L'Italie; italien c le Japon; japonaise d canadien; canadienne e anglaise f américaine g L'Espagne; espagnol h Le Luxembourg; luxembourgeoise i chinois j africaine

Exercise 74 (Unit 99): a m8 b p1 c i2 d k5 e j3 f o6 g l7 h n4

adjective an adjective is a word that describes a noun: *a long way, three great and ancient buildings.* It can be **descriptive**: *big, loud, green, gentle, contented,* etc.; **comparative**: *bigger, older, more/less big than, as big as*; **superlative**: *the biggest building, the oldest house, the most ..., the least...*; **demonstrative**: *this house, that car, these shoes, those pens*; **indefinite**: *every person, some people, certain people, several people,* etc.; **interrogative**: *which car? what event?*; **possessive**: *my office, his bike, her house,* etc.

adverb an adverb modifies a verb, an adjective or another adverb: *He ran quickly. This is a very interesting book. He writes very well.* Adverbs can also have comparative and superlative forms: *He ran more quickly (than...) He ran the quickest.*

agreement this occurs when two words have a form that indicates they have the same gender or number: *she talks, they run.*

article words meaning *the, a* or *an.* The definite article in English is *the*; the indefinite article is *a/an. Some* and *any* are partitive articles when used with non-specific nouns: *some lemonade. I haven't any paper.*

clause a group of words that contains one verb. There are main and subordinate clauses. The main clause can stand alone, the subordinate clause is dependent on it. *This is a big city* (main clause) *which I love* (subordinate clause).

comparative see **adverb** and **adjective**

compound tense tense that consists of two verb parts (auxiliary + past participle): *she has spoken.*

conjunction a conjunction can be **coordinating**, **subordinating** or **correlating**. Coordinating conjunctions link sentences, clauses, phrases or words of equal status (two main clauses, two nouns, etc): *and, but, however*, etc. Subordinating conjunctions link main and subordinate clauses: *because, although, when*, etc. Correlating conjunctions balance two or more things: *neither ... nor*.

consonant all letters of the alphabet except *a, e, i, o, u* (vowels).

conjugation see Unit 30.

gender whether a word is masculine or feminine. In French all nouns are either masculine or feminine.

impersonal verb verb without a specific subject, used in the third-person singular: *It's lovely outside.*

imperative verb form for giving orders, instructions and commands: *Turn left.*

infinitive see Unit 30.

negative word, phrase or sentence denying or contradicting something. The most common negation in English is *not*: *He couldn't find it.*

noun: a word used to name a person, an object or an abstract quality: *police officer, bank, honesty.*

number this indicates the difference between **singular** and **plural**: *one house, three houses.* In French, articles and adjectives as well as nouns show number: *les vieilles maisons.*

object the person, animal or thing that receives the action of the verb. *He ate the sandwich. They congratulated her. They sought liberty.* Objects can be direct or indirect: *I gave the book* (direct) *to her* (indirect)

partitive article these are *some*, *any* when used with nouns. *Some bread. I haven't any money.*

participle these are a form of the verb and can be present or past participles. Present participles end in *-ing* in English: *eating*. Past participles are the part of the verb used with *to have* in English: *I have eaten.*

passive form of the verb where the subject of the verb receives the action of the verb. *The day was chosen. The animals will be released.*

phrase group of words that has coherence and does not usually contain a subject and verb. It can be part of a sentence: *the way home*; *over the top*; *according to her.*

plural see **number**.

preposition word or group of words used before a noun or pronoun to show place, position, time or method: *in, on, to, from.*

pronoun word used in place of a noun or noun phrase. A pronoun can be: a **demonstrative** pronoun: *the one, this one, that one, these (ones)/those (ones)*; an **emphatic** (or **disjunctive**) pronoun: *with me, for us*; an **indefinite** pronoun: *something, someone, each one*; an **interrogative** pronoun: *who? whom? what? which one(s)?*; a **personal** pronoun (subject or direct object and indirect object pronouns): *I, he, she, it, we, you, they* (subject), *me, him, her, us, them* (direct object and indirect object); a **possessive** pronoun: *mine, his, hers,* etc.; a **relative** pronoun: *who, whom, which, that*; a **reflexive** pronoun: *myself, himself, herself,* etc. These are the object of a reflexive verb: *I wash myself.*

relative clause a clause introduced by a relative pronoun. *These are the friends who live in America.*

singular see **number**.

subject the subject of a verb is the person or object performing the action and can be a noun or pronoun. *The rain fell. They went for a sail.*

subjunctive see Unit 30.

subordinate clause see **conjunctions**.

superlative see **adverb** and **adjective**.

tense see Unit 30.

verb see Unit 30.

vowel the letters *a, e, i, o, u.*

teach yourself

french
gaëlle graham

- Do you want to cover the basics then progress fast?
- Have you got rusty French which needs brushing up?
- Do you want to reach a high standard?

French starts with the basics but moves at a lively pace to give you a good level of understanding, speaking and writing. You will have lots of opportunity to practise the kind of language you will need to be able to communicate with confidence and understand the culture of speakers of French.

french verbs
marie-thérèse weston

- Do you want a handy reference to check verb forms?
- Are you finding tenses difficult?
- Do you want to see verbs used in a variety of contexts?

French Verbs is a quick and easy way to check the form and meaning of over 3500 verbs. The clear layout makes the book very easy to navigate and the examples make the uses clear at the same time as building your vocabulary.

teach yourself®

Afrikaans
Arabic
Arabic Script, Beginner's
Bengali
Brazilian Portuguese
Bulgarian
Cantonese
Catalan
Chinese
Chinese, Beginner's
Chinese Language, Life & Culture
Chinese Script, Beginner's
Croatian
Czech
Danish
Dutch
Dutch, Beginner's
Dutch Dictionary
Dutch Grammar
English, American (EFL)
English as a Foreign Language

English, Correct
English Grammar
English Grammar (EFL)
English, Instant, for French Speakers
English, Instant, for German Speakers
English, Instant, for Italian Speakers
English, Instant, for Spanish Speakers
English for International Business
English Language, Life & Culture
English Verbs
English Vocabulary
Finnish
French
French, Beginner's
French Grammar
French Grammar, Quick Fix
French, Instant
French, Improve your
French Language, Life & Culture
French Starter Kit
French Verbs

French Vocabulary
Gaelic
Gaelic Dictionary
German
German, Beginner's
German Grammar
German Grammar, Quick Fix
German, Instant
German, Improve your
German Language, Life & Culture
German Verbs
German Vocabulary
Greek
Greek, Ancient
Greek, Beginner's
Greek, Instant
Greek, New Testament
Greek Script, Beginner's
Gulf Arabic
Hebrew, Biblical
Hindi
Hindi, Beginner's
Hindi Script, Beginner's
Hungarian
Icelandic
Indonesian
Irish
Italian
Italian, Beginner's
Italian Grammar
Italian Grammar, Quick Fix
Italian, Instant
Italian, Improve your

available from bookshops and on-line retailers

Italian Language, Life & Culture
Italian Verbs
Italian Vocabulary
Japanese
Japanese, Beginner's
Japanese, Instant
Japanese Language, Life & Culture
Japanese Script, Beginner's
Korean
Latin
Latin American Spanish
Latin, Beginner's
Latin Dictionary
Latin Grammar
Nepali
Norwegian
Panjabi
Persian, Modern
Polish
Portuguese
Portuguese, Beginner's
Portuguese Grammar
Portuguese, Instant
Portuguese Language, Life & Culture
Romanian
Russian
Russian, Beginner's
Russian Grammar
Russian, Instant
Russian Language, Life & Culture
Russian Script, Beginner's
Sanskrit
Serbian

Spanish
Spanish, Beginner's
Spanish Grammar
Spanish Grammar, Quick Fix
Spanish, Instant
Spanish, Improve your
Spanish Language, Life & Culture
Spanish Starter Kit
Spanish Verbs
Spanish Vocabulary
Swahili
Swahili Dictionary
Swedish
Tagalog
Teaching English as a Foreign Language
Teaching English One to One
Thai
Turkish
Turkish, Beginner's
Ukrainian
Urdu
Urdu Script, Beginner's
Vietnamese
Welsh
Welsh Dictionary
Welsh Language, Life & Culture
Xhosa
Zulu